SARAH: A Sexual Biography

SUNY Series in Sexual Behavior

DONN BYRNE *and* KATHRYN KELLEY, *Editors*

SARAH

A Sexual Biography

BY PAUL R. ABRAMSON

State University of New York Press, Albany

Published by
State University of New York Press, Albany

For information, address State University of New York Press,
90 State Street, Suite 700, Albany, NY 12207

Library of Congress Cataloging in Publication Data

Abramson, Paul R., 1949–
   Sarah, a sexual biography.

   (SUNY series in sexual behavior)
   Includes bibliographical references.
   1. Incest victims—Case studies. 2. Sexually abused
children—Case studies. I. Title. II. Series.
RC560.I53A27   1984   306.7'77'0926   83-17983
ISBN 0-87395-862-4
ISBN 0-87395-863-2 (pbk.)

To Sarah, a constant source of amazement;
to Carnohan, for your support and enthusiasm;
and to my brother Keith, who aptly advised,
"You can drive off that bridge when you get to it."

CONTENTS

PROLOGUE

The Role of Case Histories in Psychosexology

DONN BYRNE and KATHRYN KELLEY

State University of New York at Albany

Accidental events frequently turn out better than well planned ones. We contacted Paul Abramson in January of 1983 about the possibility of writing a book or chapter dealing with the assessment of sexual arousal. He expressed interest but informed us that he had a quite different kind of manuscript already completed, the sexual biography of a female college student. It may be seen that we contacted him without knowing that he had this book in hand, and he wrote it without knowing that Dr. Susan Suarez would be asking us to serve as editors of a new publishing venture for a university press. So, none of us can claim responsibility for the way in which it developed, but it is particularly appropriate that a case history constitutes the initial volume in the SUNY Press series on Sexual Behavior.

There is increasing reason to believe that psychosexology is finally coming of age as a science (see Byrne, 1977a, 1982; Davis, 1983), and we are justly proud of today's sophisticated research techniques, growing data base, and developing theoretical formulations. It should be remembered, however, that the enterprise began with descriptions and interpretations of the behavior of individuals such as "Sarah." What can be learned from the exposure of the intimate details of one person's life experiences? No two case histories are exactly alike, and the story of Sarah is unlike any other that we have read. Nevertheless, this approach to understanding human behavior can be placed in a general context that applies to all case

3

histories. Such a context allows us to appreciate the general characteristics of the case history method, its limitations, and the unique
contributions it can make.

A Slice of Life: The First Steps toward
Understanding Sexual Behavior

In the task of understanding and controlling physical illness, a
familiar historical progression has been to identify and to describe
minutely the detailed symptoms of a given ailment, to seek its
causes, and to ascertain its future course with and without appropriate treatment. At the end of the nineteenth century, numerous
medical specialists turned their attention from physical disabilities
to emotional and behavioral problems. Not surprisingly, they
adopted the prevailing medical approach and proceeded to describe
behavioral anomalies, to speculate about their possible physiolog-
ical and experiential antecedents, and to establish prognostic proba-
bilities. Almost all of the succeeding accounts of individual human
behavior, including the one of Sarah, tend to fit within such a pattern—whether written by physicians, psychologists, or social
workers.

In the transition from physical to psychological concerns, it soon
became obvious that the description of fever, skin eruptions, or the
site of a severe pain was qualitatively different from describing the
life experiences of a maladjusted individual. For one thing, it was
necessary to borrow the techniques and even the style of novelists,
biographers, historians, and anthropologists. Freud quickly recognized these aspects of his newly developing profession. In a letter
to his fiancée in 1884, he wrote that he was "becoming aware of literary stirrings when previously I could not have imagined anything
further from my mind." He extended this theme in *Studies in Hysteria* when he noted, "It still strikes me as strange that the case histories I write should read like short stories and that, as one might say,
they lack the serious stamp of science."

In addition to their literary aspects, behavioral case histories
present the problem of having essentially limitless boundaries. A

medical description is circumscribed by an individual's body and its functioning. A psychological description can conceivably include anything and everything that a person has experienced, felt, imagined, desired, dreamed, or anticipated. There is obviously no way for the observer to know when to stop; the story can never be complete.

These psychological studies differ from medical descriptions in a third way. There is a pervasive subjectivity in the account, both as provided by the subject and as perceived and organized by the observer. Think for a moment of what you can remember and what you are willing to disclose to someone else about any event in your life from your first sexual encounter to what you did last week. What would you say, what words would you use, what might you decide to omit, and what might you exaggerate just a bit? Under the best of circumstances, our memories can be inaccurate and partially distorted by our knowledge of more recent events (Snyder & Uranowitz, 1978). Consider also what analogous distortions might be imposed by someone who listened to your story and made it availale to others. It may be concluded that subjectivity is an integral part of any case history.

Despite the limitations inherent in this method, the result is almost always much more engaging than any analogous description of measles, appendicitis, or AIDS. When an individual has a history as unusual as that of Sarah, with a multitude of experiences in both childhood and adolescence unlike those most of us encounter in a lifetime, the resulting case history is more than just engaging. It is a penetrating view of a set of circumstances that are more horrendous and more involving than the content of even the most vivid fiction. It should be added that the artistry of both the person telling her story and of the psychologist presenting it to us is an essential component that helps to make this material fascinating to any reader.

Detailed behavioral case histories have an additional component; few life stories can be complete without including sexuality. Anyone who reads these accounts is exposed to a first- (or second-) hand description of the sexual lives of others. Because everyday sexual behavior is ordinarily hidden from public view and avoided as a topic of conversation at family gatherings, for many people such presentations provide their first information about the sexual proclivities of anyone beyond themselves or (to a lesser degree) their partners. At times, it is difficult to appreciate how relatively recent these developments have been in Western civilization. When Samuel Pepys began his *Diary* on the first day of 1660, he decided to include as much detail as possible, from financial dealings to sexual episodes; the latter material was omitted from the published versions until the present decade (Hill, 1983). Even today, one can easily react with surprise, amazement, or even disgust when reading about someone very different from oneself in his or her sexual inclinations and practices.

With these considerations as background, we can examine the sexual case histories of the nineteenth and twentieth centuries and appreciate their significance. We can also identify the commonalities linking the partly fictionalized autobiographical accounts of *My Secret Life* (Anonymous, 1966), *The Thief's Journal* (Genet, 1964), *My Life and Loves* (Harris, 1958), and *Tropic of Cancer* (Miller, 1961) with the clinical accounts of Krafft-Ebing (1894), Ellis (1936), Freud (1962), and many others.

The cumulative effect of the availability of private sexual histories on behavioral science and even on everyday behavior is difficult or impossible to assess. It may be that the vast changes over recent decades in sexual research as well as in sexual attitudes, behavior, and tolerance (Hunt, 1974) are partially a function of the growing awareness of what it is that others feel and believe and do. There is no conclusive way to solve the problem of the chicken versus the egg, but we do know that dramatic societal changes have taken place and are associated with the widespread availability of explicit sexual case histories as well as analogous novels, movies, magazines, plays, and so forth (Byrne, 1977b). Without necessarily praising or condemning the changes, we might agree that the presence of such verbal and pictorial images serves to instruct, expand our knowledge, warn us of pitfalls, and probably, over time, to desensitize us (Byrne, 1977c). The possibility is suggested, then, that these sexual revelations have an unexpected and unintended role in society as agents of change.

Altogether, case histories may be viewed as a pioneering technique in opening up the study of human sexual behavior and perhaps (along with many other events) in ushering in revolutionary changes in attitudes and behavior. Beyond that, what is the scientific contribution of this material? Are case histories little more than a socially acceptable way to peer through a stranger's bedroom window in search of titillating secrets, or do they provide a legitimate and useful source of knowledge? We will briefly examine the weaknesses and the strengths of this source of sexual information.

The Limitations of an Individual's Life Story as a Source of Scientific Data

Perhaps the most striking feature of even a detailed account such as that of Sarah is the way in which different observers can reach widely divergent conclusions about its accuracy and its meaning. D. M. Thomas's (1981) novel, *The White Hotel*, provides a convincing demonstration of the slippery slopes of truth in any such undertaking. Among those who read Sarah's account prior to its publication, the reactions have ranged from the assumption of its base in fiction rather than fact to a belief in its absolute truthfulness. Perceptions of Sarah's present psychological state range from Professor Abramson's assessment of her remarkably good adjustment as the happy survivor of a traumatic past to an equally able reviewer's assessment that she may be a manipulative and seductive young woman driven by narcissism, sadism, and masochism. Which perception is correct? Or, is some other view more accurate than either of these? The answer, of course, is that no one knows for sure. For the scientist, a case history can provide new information and serve as the source of ideas. It can be the stimulus for the creation of original hypotheses. Except in the aggregate, however, case histories can represent only a preliminary step in the scientific process. This limitation should be remembered as one examines Sarah's story.

One way to describe scientific activity is as a series of processes beginning with observation, progressing to a more abstract level of generalization, proceeding to hypothesis-testing that can verify or disconfirm one's generalizations, and culminating in theory-building that guides us to additional observations, generalizations, hypothesis-testing, and extensions or modifications of the theory (Byrne & Kelley, 1981). With case histories, it is the *testing of hypotheses* that is missing. An essential element in the scientific method is the panoply of procedures that have evolved to allow us to identify useful concepts that generate accurate predictions. Such predictive accuracy, in turn, allows us to use our conceptualizations for desirable applications. In a sense, empirical science "keeps us honest" in our speculations as we determine what can be verified, what cannot be verified, and even what is unverifiable.

When a case history provides us with a series of observations that we could not otherwise have made and if it leads us to ideas about behavior that might not otherwise have occurred, it can be a fertile source for constructing a science of behavior (Holt, 1962). In contrast, when anyone jumps directly to theory without pausing for data collection, the result is an array of infinitely arguable alternatives. The image is that of bar patrons debating about which animal is our best friend or of personality theorists early in this century debating the fine points of psychic structure and functioning. Only empirical science can cut through the verbal fog by specifying what is meant in operational terms, designing relevant controlled observations, manipulating conditions whenever possible, quantifying variables, and utilizing inferential statistics. These are among the self-correcting mechanisms that separate science from endless speculation and from a multitude of nonscientific procedures that also attempt to make sense out of the world around us.

One reviewer noted that Professor Abramson interspersed the account of Sarah with interpretations that elicited a reaction of "Wait a minute." In other words, "How does he know that's true without putting it to an empirical test?" We feel confident that anyone with Paul Abramson's research record would agree. It would be cumbersome for the author to verbalize this each time a comment is offered, but each such interpretation should be considered to be an hypothesis to be evaluated in future research and not as a final conclusion carved in stone.

The Unique Contribution of One Individual's
Story

We have suggested the utility of case histories as a source of
ideas. Howe (1982) has pointed out another advantage. Autobiographical or biographical material consists of many different observations made over a relatively lengthy period of time. This long-
range perspective of development and change cannot be duplicated
by a very limited number of observations in an experiment or in a
testing session. When detailed case histories of multiple individuals
are examined, it becomes possible to identify common antecedents
for particular consequents. In this way, case histories provide very
useful data to supplement our more familiar research observations
(Block, 1971; White, 1975).

In addition to long-term developmental observations, the practi-
tioner who utilizes "intensive local observation" to seek compre-
hension of phenomena will be alert to accumulations of data that
lead to meaningful generalizations and to equally important excep-
tions to those generalizations (Cronbach, 1975). As Barlow (1981)
points out, this process gives us access to the responses of specific
individuals in a designated natural setting—information that cannot be provided by traditional laboratory investigations. Direct observation of individuals generates data that are different from but
potentially complementary to the products of theoretically based ex-
perimentation.

There is still another positive aspect to examining the details of
one person's life. It is a truism that most of us would readily stop to
assist a frightened child who was crying out for help, though we
might remain relatively unmoved by a news account of 5,000 or-
phans perishing in an earthquake. What is the difference? Why do
we cry at the death of an individual and simply nod resignedly
when we learn that "only" 120,000,000 Americans would be killed
in a full-scale nuclear exchange?

The difference seems to be that we can identify and empathize
with a specific individual. We respond emotionally and perceive
that person as a human being like ourselves. In neurophysiological

terms, the limbic system and the right hemisphere of the cortex are involved. That is, we respond affectively, and we recognize the pattern of another human's life as an aesthetic whole (Gazzaniga, 1967, 1970; Robinson, 1973). When confronted with the abstraction of large numbers or summary statistics, it is the left hemisphere of the cortex that is operative. There is sequential processing of information, but we remain objective observers rather than sympathetic participants. It is the difference between an emotional response to a work of art and an intellectual response to the stock listings in today's paper. Holt (1962) proposed the term "literary biography" for the artistic aspect of personality psychology. A major concern is the effect on the audience, an "illumination," something to which science may remain indifferent.

This, then, is the unique contribution of a case history such as that of Sarah. Her story of sexual abuse by her stepfather and stepbrother is very likely to elicit a very different, more personal, and longer-lasting response in the reader than could ever be gained from a careful, large-scale investigation of incest and exhaustive documentation of the frequency with which children are sexually exploited. It is not that one sort of information is more valuable than the other; rather, it is the fact that these different sources elicit different responses. Both provide elements of understanding, and case histories should be valued for what they do best and not dismissed for their failure to provide what they cannot.

Sarah's story can give each of us an intimate view of a very special life and lead us to valuable speculations as to how she managed to reach her present state following a seemingly devastating childhood and adolescence. We can try to understand why she and her sister managed to reach such different outcomes. An optimal benefit for behavioral science would be any research that is generated by those who are moved, intrigued, puzzled, or even skeptical about this young woman's sexual history.

REFERENCES

ANONYMOUS. (1966). *My secret life*. New York: Grove Press. (Original work published 1888)

BARLOW, D. H. (1981). On the relation of clinical research to clinical practice: Current issues, new directions. *Journal of Consulting and Clinical Psychology, 49,* 147–155.

BLOCK J. (1971). *Lives through time.* Berkeley, CA: Bancroft.

BYRNE, D. (1977a). Social psychology and the study of sexual behavior. *Personality and Social Psychology Bulletin, 3,* 3–30.

BYRNE, D. (1977b). Sexual changes in society and in science. In D. Byrne & L. A. Byrne (Eds.), *Exploring human sexuality* (pp. 12–23). New York: Harper and Row.

BYRNE, D. (1977c). The imagery of sex. In J. Money & H. Musaph (Eds.), *Handbook of sexology* (pp. 327–50). Amsterdam: Excerpta Medica.

BYRNE, D., & KELLY, K. (1981). *An introduction to personality* (3rd ed.). Englewood Cliffs, NJ: Prentice-Hall.

CRONBACH, L. J. (1975). Beyond the two disciplines of scientific psychology. *American Psychologist, 30,* 116–27.

DAVIS, C. M. (Ed.). (1983). *Challenges in sexual science: Current theoretical issues and research advances.* Syracuse: Society for the Scientific Study of Sex.

ELLIS, H. (1936). *Studies in the psychology of sex.* New York: Random House. (Original work published 1899)

FREUD, S. (1962). *Three contributions to the theory of sex.* New York: Dutton. (Original work published 1905)

GAZZANIGA, M. S. (1967). The split brain in man. *Scientific American, 217,* 24–29.

GAZZANIGA, M. S. (1970). *The bisected brain.* Englewood Cliffs, NJ: Prentice-Hall.

GENET, J. (1964). *The thief's journal.* New York: Grove Press. (Original work published 1949)

HARRIS, F. (1958). *My life and loves.* Paris: Olympia Press.

HILL, C. (1983). Pepys show. *The New Republic, 189* (1), 25–28.

HOLT, R. R. (1962). Individuality and generalization in the psychology of personality. *Journal of Personality, 30,* 377–404.

HOWE, M. J. A. (1982). Biographical evidence and the development of outstanding individuals. *American Psychologist, 37,* 1071–81.

HUNT, M. (1974). *Sexual behavior in the 1970s.* Chicago: Playboy Press.

KRAFFT-EBING, R. VON. (1894). *Psychopathia sexualis.* Philadelphia: F. A. Davis. (Original work published 1886)

MILLER, H. (1965). *Tropic of cancer.* New York: Grove Press.

ROBINSON, D. N. (1973). *The enlightened machine.* Encino, CA: Dickenson.

SNYDER, M., & URANOWITZ, S. W. (1978). Reconstructing the past: Some cognitive consequences of person perception. *Journal of Personality and Social Psychology, 36,* 941–50.

THOMAS, D. M. (1981). *The white hotel.* New York: Viking Press.

WHITE, R. W. (1975). *Lives in progress: A study of the natural growth of personality* (3rd ed.). New York: Holt, Rinehart and Winston.

SARAH

Introduction

This is a true story. Despite containing all of the elements of a grade B movie (adversity, tragedy, intrigue, and finally, triumph) this case is nonetheless significant because it bears testimony to psychological survival. And the purpose of this book is to understand how Sarah did it.

The orientation of this book is *cognitive-existential*.[1] It is cognitive in the sense that it tries to reconstruct Sarah's thinking. Attention is paid to the formation of Sarah's identity, based upon her expression of thoughts, feelings, and experiences. It is also existential in that it examines how Sarah created meaning out of her life, despite the abuse and trauma.

On January 4, 1979, I received the following unsolicited letter* from a former student, whom I barely knew:

> December 23, 1978
> Paris, France

Dear Dr. Abramson:

Today is my 21st birthday and I am taking my first breaths of "adulthood." Birthdays can be a useful time for reflection and renewal, and 21 years marks an especially important point in most

---

1. E. Becker, *The denial of death* (New York: Free Press, 1973); and E. Becker, *The structure of evil* (New York: Braziller, 1968).

*All of Sarah's material is being quoted verbatim.

occidental societies. Being 21 means that I am now old enough to purchase alcoholic beverages in the state of California, that I am no longer under the auspices of my grandparents financial support, that I no longer see my psychologist (in a clinical setting), and that I inherit some ridiculous amount of money.

When taking a general look at the miasma that lies behind me from the age of 16 to now, my own mind boggles. My fair youth doesn't seem to be rich in the experiences that are generally considered normal adolescent behavior. At 16 I moved away from home, was a handsomely paid prostitute for about 5 months, smoked excessively, took numerous drugs, and had hundreds of various love affairs. During the past 5 years I have also had 2 major peak experiences, gone through self-rehabilitation, have seen 2 therapists, have withdrawn myself from the arena of bisexuality, have been pregnant twice, painfully close to marriage once, and have been to Europe 5 times. To top off all this, on the plane from L.A. to London I seduced this very sweet Swedish man in the bathroom at the back of the plane. It was one of those just-for-the-hell-of-it experiences, but in retrospect it was very anti-climatic.

So much for the past. To continue my discussion of birthdays, my birthday holds a special significance to me, as I'm sure they do for many. I was born near the darkest day of the year which coincided wth the darkest night of the month, the winter solstice and the new moon. It isn't as dismal as it sounds. In the Chinese Book of Changes the winter solstice "brings the victory of light," and the new moon marks also the end of darkness and the waning of light. They are symbolic turning points.

This letter is a kind of document of reflection at the 21 year turning point and for some reason, unbeknownst to me, I feel inspired to share it with you. My doctor friend's lecture was rescheduled for today, so I'm taking some fruit and cheese to the little island of Saint Helier off the coast here to spend the day. There's a lovely monastery there and the atmosphere is most conducive to further reflection.

Your friend,
"Sarah"

Of course I found the letter striking. Whether the intention was to shock me or gain my sympathy, it ultimately got my attention. Which may have been its purpose.

On February 7, 1979, Sarah dropped by my office, unannounced.

It did not surprise her that I remembered the letter. She appeared nervous and avoided eye contact. I asked her if she would permit me to tape record her life history for a case study. She agreed, was assured of anonymity, and signed the requisite release forms.

At our first interview Sarah was much less reserved. I made it clear to her that this was not psychotherapy. I told her that if she preferred psychotherapy I would make a referral. She laughed and said that she had had enough therapists. I also made it clear to Sarah that she could stop at anytime, or withdraw from the project. I was soon to learn that of the two of us, she was the more diligent.

This last sentence may surprise some readers. I mean, what did Sarah get out of this? To be quite honest, I am not sure. My guess is that it was important for her to tell her life, uncensored and without interruption. In a way, it was her confession. It is also clear that she received complete, yet tacit approval from me. That is, I accepted her throughout her story. Sarah also indicated that while some of this material was discussed during the course of her previous therapy, it was never presented in such detail, or with such continuity.

My first impression of Sarah was that she was both passive and depressive. She was also highly intelligent and quite articulate. Sarah seemed to blunder into relationships, using shock and masochism as her calling cards. Shock was manifested in her tendency to be outrageous, and masochism was apparent in the object of her outrageousness, i.e., Sarah. Her contact with me is consistent with this pattern. She sparked interest through her notoriety, yet needed to abuse herself, be abused, or *talk* about her abuse, in order to connect with people.

I spent six months interviewing Sarah. The interviews occurred once a week, and were approximately one hour in duration. Sarah also provided me with several hundred pages of her diary, photographs of people who were significant in her life, and an occasional dream. This convergence of data is quite unusual for a psychological case study. However, each data source has its limitations. I was careful to repeat questions throughout the interviews so as to check the continuity of her story. I also interviewed a previous fiancé to obtain corroborating testimony.

I let three years elapse before writing this book. I felt I needed periodic follow-ups to strengthen my conclusions. During that time I also attended her wedding, where I met most of the people discussed in the book. I also spent time with her before and after her first child. Finally, we corresponded while I was on sabbatical at Kyoto University, Japan. What follows is her narrative, mixed with my interpretations and reconstructions, samples from her diaries, examples of her drawings, descriptions of the photographs, and occasional dreams.

SARAH

My father is an engineer and he now lives in San Francisco. He is a pessimistic, old frustrated hippie. He divorced my mother when I was four. I guess he didn't want to be married. The only reason they got married was because she was pregnant with me. I think he was going to California Technological Institute at the time, and my mother was going to Berkeley. My father eventually dropped out to make money.

Once he was married, he became very dissatisfied, wanting to be a bachelor instead. Supposedly, he told the divorce lawyer that being married cramped his style. He wanted to go out, and a family didn't fit in somehow. For some reason, the divorce lawyer thought this was great, and decided not to work against my father. So my parents just split up. Actually, my mother didn't get an official divorce until she decided to marry my stepfather.

After my father left, I didn't see him very much until I was seventeen. I loved my father, but we didn't get along. He was a very proud, and a very negative person.

The few times that I saw my father, when I was very young, were very strange. He had this theory that incest with your children is okay. Incest with anybody in your family was okay. I think that he had so much trouble relating to the outside world, that the family was his own built-in system of nourishment, sexual or otherwise. To him, that was just a wonderful thing. He was all into the sexual revolution.

Talking about this is very difficult. I've never told anybody about my father. I've told them about my stepbrother; I've told them about my stepfather; but I've never told anybody about my father because I knew that they wouldn't understand his approach.

I don't know exactly when the incest with my father started. I think the seeds of it were always there. I never liked it when my father gave me a bath, especially when I was four or five, visiting him in San Francisco. I don't know, it was strange, I wasn't a very physical child. I didn't like to be touched a lot, or bossed around. He did both.

Certain things are not vivid in my mind when I visited him. One of the things that I *do* remember is that although I never saw my mother go to the bathroom, I saw my father go. In fact I'd imitate him at the toilet. He wasn't impressed. I also remember that my sister and I and my father all slept in the same bed. My sister Karen is about a year younger than I am, and is another "mistake." Karen and I used to inspect my father's genitals while he lay in bed reading. Not having a penis myself, I was very impressed. And I remember being in awe at the folds of skin which could cover his penis. When I would roll it down, there would be something new.

When I was around nine, the incest intensified. When I would wake up, my father would be touching my breasts and genitals, while he had an erection. It always seemed like a very strange position to be in. I really didn't know what I was supposed to be doing. Something felt wrong to me. I very often pretended like I was asleep. It was the easiest thing I could do. I could pretend like nothing was happening. I think a few times I got up and went to the bathroom and didn't come back until later. Yet . . . I didn't feel any discomfort with this, although it seemed incongruent. Also, I didn't feel frightened or disgusted.

Later, when I was seventeen, I talked with my father about this. I told him that I didn't want him as a lover. I would prefer he'd be a better father. Fortunately, all of this stopped when I was around thirteen. By that time, I had sex with a boyfriend, so it felt even worse. It really felt . . . wrong. Also awkward, and strange.

Earthquakes are terrifying because they challenge one of our most cherished beliefs, i.e., the earth is hard and stable. Incestuous parents are terrifying for the same reason, they challenge our need for stable, nourishing, and munificent caretakers. Sarah's father is a good example of this challenge. Whatever warmth and care he gave to his children is countered by his transgressions. Children are naive, but not that naive. And Sarah's narrative is testimony to the confusion it created. First, note that Sarah vacillates between condoning her father and condemning him, and between expressing nonchalance and describing her trauma. When a parent oversteps parental boundaries, children are immediately confused as to the parent's role. Parents and children do not have sex. If a parent has sex with a child, is the parent still a parent? Most children avoid trying to solve this confusion by repressing the incestual experiences. Unfortunately, repression is a poor defense because the repressed material keeps coming back to consciousness. A clue to Sarah's eventual success and adjustment is perhaps the fact that she did not repress these experiences from herself.

Sarah's photos of her father (which are labeled "Daddy-O") are quite striking. In the late 1960s he looks like a cowboy hustler, à la Jon Voight in *Midnight Cowboy*. His long thinning blond hair is combed straight back; his sideburns are two inches below his ears; and his piercing blue eyes and high cheekbones give him a raw and ravaged look. He also sports a cowboy hat in one picture.

Although Sarah's experiences with her father are alarming, they are pale in comparison with the abuse she received from her stepbrother, stepfather, and mother. What follows is her narrative of those experiences:

My first real encounters with sex occurred when I was five years old—with my stepbrother and stepfather. When I was five, my stepbrother was twelve, and he would come to stay with us for a while. (He had been living with his mother.) He was really obnoxious . . . really horrible. He used to beat Karen and I up a lot. He would also break things around the house and blame them on us.

Anyway, one of the things my stepbrother Karl used to do was to lock me in the bathroom with him. He told me that if I made any noise he'd punch me in the face. I wasn't too eager to make any noise. He would then take his finger and stick it in my vagina really hard . . . and I was only five years old—and it used to . . . it was extremely painful. I used to scream and cry and get upset. I even threatened to tell my mother but he would start to choke me. I never caught on that my mother would be suspicious if she found us in the bathroom together. It never occurred to me that two kids were not supposed to be in the bathroom at the same time.

Much worse things happened with my stepfather. In fact, this is one of my most vivid memories . . . because at the time . . . I had no idea of what was going on. I remember him (his name was Al) waking me up and telling me to come into the living room. It was very late and my mother was asleep in the bedroom. Actually, she would sleep in the bedroom, and he would sleep in the living room. (This part really makes me sick. It's funny, it's not the physical act that makes me sick, it's the things he said that turn my stomach.) When Al woke me up he said,

"Do you want some Italian sausage?" I didn't know what he was talking about so I said, "Sure." He then took his pants off and he made me touch his penis. Next, he made me put my mouth around his penis . . . and I was getting very sick. He then came. I thought it was urine, but it doesn't make any difference. I didn't particularly care. I was being tortured . . . I just felt sick. He then told me not tell my mother.

The next morning my mother asked me why I was so sleepy. I didn't think anything of it, so I told her exactly what happened. However, I didn't expect the reaction I got. I remember that she didn't say anything at all; she was just looking out the window. And I kept checking with her to find out what was wrong . . . what's going on? She didn't say anything so I asked her if I said something horrible.

Years later, my mother told me that she talked to my stepfather. He had told her it was "a young child's imagination." I have a sense that she wanted to believe that. She came from a rather sheltered Jewish-American Princess background. I think she found it hard to believe that it could have happened in the first place. I think it was too much conflict for her. And of course she wanted to believe her new husband. As a result . . . it kept going on, and I kept telling her about it.

As I got older, it got worse. I can directly remember him trying to enter me when I was eleven. By eleven years old, I had already menstruated. Also, he would spend a lot of time touching my breasts, which he called "chi chi's." That word makes me sick. After a night of this, the next morning I would be sleepy, exhausted, and generally kind of sick. However, he would always be very helpful and very sweet to me. He usually wasn't this way. He was horrible. To Karen and I it was like living with the devil.

Karen and I were beaten by Al a lot. Usually it was for made-up things. I remember once the plug to the bathtub was missing. And he knew that he had lost it. Yet he had this huge explosion. He's a very big man, about 6'2". He was also a boxer, with a punched-in nose. I remember another time when I was nine years old, and cleaning up the house. Al had left a dirty watering can in the house, but started yelling at Karen and I. "How could you do something like that?" . . . screaming and yelling, "You're a rotten child—just like your mother." He also called us whores. . . "You're a whore, just like your mother." It was really wonderful.

I started running away a lot. I had a bicycle so I would ride away. And as soon as I would get back, an explosion would start, so I would leave again. This was when I was eleven. It was also at this time that my mother walked into the room while Al was in bed with me. He had gotten into the habit of just walking in, taking his pants off and climbing into bed. The worse of it was that he would never keep his mouth shut. He would say sickening things like, "You're a much better woman than your mother," "You're going to make a wonderful wife sometime," "Keep your legs straight," "Don't put your hands over your breasts," "Let me touch your chi-chis."

I was terrified of this man. When he would start screaming I would become paralyzed. I couldn't do anything. If asked a question, I probably wouldn't be able to answer. Anyway . . . when my mother came in this time, she started screaming at him, "All these years you've been *lying* about this!" You know, that was one of the things that absolutely shocked me—that my mother didn't believe *me*. I mean like, all those years, *I* could be making it up.

Of course, Al started yelling, "I wasn't doing anything. Is it wrong for a father to show his daughter a little affection?" Meanwhile, he didn't even bother to get out of bed with me, so my mother left. When she left, he started in all over again.

I think my mother just went and drove somewhere. She was extremely passive. You know . . . she could have taken me with her. But she just left, and I was stuck with him. When my mother found him in bed with me, she asked me if he had done anything. I was so scared that I said no. Here he is with his arms around me, but I was too paralyzed to qualify that. What I meant was that nothing is going on *yet*. But when she left, he then proceeded.

He told me to take off my clothes and spread my legs. He tried to enter me that night. But it was very painful. However, it wasn't as painful as I made it sound. I tried to make it sound as painful as possible. Finally my stepfather left. He never did have intercourse with me.

Oftentimes I wouldn't do anything. I would just lay there. I guess I was very wishy-washy. But I was afraid to sleep alone, even though I liked to, because Al would always come in. So I would sleep with Karen. I thought there was less a chance of him doing anything with her around. Actually, Karen once walked in when Al was in bed with me. She had this blank expression on her face. He didn't say anything to her. He didn't have to; he had us intimidated with all of his screaming.

How does someone survive a hell like this? The answer is they usually don't. As you will see later, while Sarah made it, Karen did not.

Human cruelty takes many forms: war atrocities, murder, rape, kidnapping, and so on. In each case the tormentor pursues the victim—and the victim tries to escape. But what if the tormentor is the child's parent? And he or she doesn't want to escape, because where else will you go, and who will believe you? Sexual abuse of children is one of the most heinous crimes because the child is ultimately dependent upon the tormentor. It is a "no-win" situation. Given ample freedom to escape, most abused children are doomed to stay in place because they usually believe that there is no other place to go.

Al is a cruel, sick, and pathetic man who should be tried for these crimes. I did not meet him, but from his pictures he looks like a mean, dumb gangster. A big thick forehead, with small eyes and a punched-in nose, he resembles mugshots from the "FBI Most Wanted List." But as bad as his crimes were, Sarah's mother's neglect is nearly as reprehensible. At the first sign of sexual abuse, she should have left Al. Instead, she perpetuated the misery through her inertia. In some cases, mothers feign ignorance to serve their own needs. Mother can withdraw from father by using daughter as a substitute. In this particular case, it is not clear to what extent this dynamic was operating. Sarah's mother is a very frail and passive-looking woman with long brown hair and a prominent nose. In person, she appears slightly warmer, yet has a vacant look in her eyes.

Sarah's stepbrother was cruel, just like his father. And for Sarah, this home life provided little consolation from the never-ending trauma. Unfortunately, the abuse was more than sexual, it was an assiduous attempt to undermine the psychology of a little girl. Sarah's narrative continues:

> Al had an identity for each of us. Karen was the "dummy." She had some problems as a child which they thought were epilepsy. But she didn't have epilepsy, the environment was just stifling. However, she did have problems reading. Under these circumstances, that wasn't unusual. Yes . . . her identity was the dummy, the stupid one, the one who doesn't know anything.
>
> I was the liar, the cheater, the schemer. I guess I got that identity because I was always trying to tell my mother to leave him. Whenever she was close to leaving

him, I was there saying, "Let's go! Let's get in the car right now!" So, I was the enemy.

I don't think Al had incest with Karen. But I'm not sure about my father. My father had stronger feelings toward her than toward me, although he used to get very jealous of my boyfriends. I once tried to talk with Karen about this, telling her what I went through with our father. She said she had been through the same thing. I think my father was attracted to Karen because she looks like my mother, and acts like my mother. My father is still very fond of Karen.

Even though my mother caught Al with me, she still stayed with him. However she finally threw him out when I left home with Karen. I was only eleven at the time, but I would take Karen and go stay with neighbors. I then told this neighbor what was going on. But I didn't let this neighbor go to the police. I was afraid of getting my mother in trouble. I don't know why I thought that. But I was very protective of my mother. I loved my mother very much . . . I wanted everything to be just like it was before Al came.

My mother is a wonderful person, but she's crazy. These things go hand in hand. She loved nature a lot. She loved animals. We used to go on camping trips and go to places to pick wild flowers. She would just pack up the van, with dogs and kids. It's funny, she was really a wonderful mother, until she met Al.

My mother never hit us. Whenever there was something she wanted us to do, she would sit us down and tell us. If there were things that I didn't understand, she would show me diagrams, pictures, books, maps, and things. It was real nice.

However, when she got married to Al, we didn't get very much attention. She was busy catering to him. He didn't work. She met him at the race track. The two of them were betting on horses. He had found out from my mother's cousin that my mother had a lot of money. My mother was so gullible. Even as a child I knew how easy it was to trick her. I'd see people doing it all the time. If someone told her a sad story, she would immediately give them something, or do something for them. She still does that, but not quite as bad. But my stepfather, he told her *so much bullshit*. I mean even at nine years old, *I* knew it was bullshit.

You see, my mother was a spoiled only child. Her parents are very, very wealthy and live in Beverly Hills. She was raised by a governess. These grandparents are Jewish, and they were very frightened that Hitler was going to come over to this country and take their only daughter away. So they got this young French governess to raise my mother as a Catholic. In this way, if Hitler came over, the governess could say that my mother was *her* child— and my mother in turn could tell them about Catholicism. Actually, every time I am disappointed by my mother, I attribute it to her being raised as a Catholic, in a Jewish home.

Al was also Catholic (of Italian descent). In many ways my mother was continuing her Catholicism by marrying another Catholic. But it was all for the worse. Besides the incest, we were beaten a lot. We were beaten with belts, shoes, hangers and cords . . . anything you could think of. And our bodies showed it. In fact, my real father took us to the police department to show them what my stepfather had done to us. I remember him making us show the police the bruises and marks we had from the hangers. But my father had trouble making a point of this. You know . . . it is only recently that child beating has become a big issue. Also, when Al finally went down to the police station, he just charmed the cops: "Oh, they did this and that, and I just got a little mad at her. That's all."

I was glad my father stepped in. It helps me feel better about him today. In fact, I now think that we have a good relationship. Fortunately, he has calmed down a lot—he's not very old, only forty-four. Yet he acts like he's sixty-five or something. Perhaps it's because he just went back to work as an engineer. When he left my mother, he "retired," and hung out around Haight-Ashbury. He lived very modestly, doing odd jobs here and there. One of his jobs was selling penis-shaped candles, which he designed. He called his "company" "Ding-Dong Candle Works." It didn't go very far. One summer, when we went to visit him, there were pink, yellow, and red, white, and blue phallic candles everywhere. Some had little lights that blinked on and off. He actually got arrested for this. I think he sent a candle to President Nixon. I have a picture of him peddling these candles. But once he got arrested, he gave it up.

It's funny, when he was selling those candles, he was into the protesting scene around San Francisco. In fact, he used to send news clippings to me. I guess he still wanted to be a father even if he was far away . . . and sending us books and articles and things to read was as close as he wanted to get. I actually have pictures of him in protest lines, charging through police barricades. I think this was a very interesting period of time for him.

Although my mother threw my stepfather out when I was eleven, the divorce didn't become final until I was fourteen. Unfortunately, Al used to come back in the interim. He would come in, and say that he was sick or something . . . and my mother would let him stay there for a few days. And a few days would turn into a few weeks, and a few weeks into a few months. Then something would happen . . . he'd explode, and Karen and I would leave. So even after the time my mother walked into my bedroom, Al was still allowed to come back. As I said before, I don't think that it was the incest per se which made her throw him out.

Besides being tragic, Sarah's family life was incredibly convoluted. Her father is a good example. Here is this incestuous, but absent parent, bringing his abused children to the police to compalin about an incredibly cruel and incestuous stepparent. The father is an aging hippie who makes his living selling penis-shaped candles, and the stepfather is a vicious-looking gambler with no visible means of support. To top it off, Sarah's mother is ineffectual and noncommittal, though she seems capable of pleasing her children when she is entertaining them with picnics and hikes.

It is not surprising that Sarah's feelings are equally convoluted. She has love/hate relationships with her father and mother, alternating her description of them between positive characteristics and negative characteristics. Only her stepfather receives uniform wrath. However, these feelings are appropriate. Despite their limitations and abuse, her mother and father did provide support and love. Her stepfather, on the other hand, was without any redeeming qualities.

It is often easier to forgive when we interpret someone's intentions as being benign. Sarah forgives her father because she believes that his sexual abuse was rooted in a philosophy which was patently absurd. The "sexual revolution" permits freedom of sexual expression—and to extend it to one's children is a bizarre, but excusable offense (at least according to Sarah). Sarah's father did little to hide his commitment to sexual politics. Besides sending Sarah clippings of his exploits, she also has a picture of him displaying his "Ding-Dong Candles." As she indicated, he had designed and produced candles in the shape of an erection, with the testicles and scrotum acting as a base. Out of each urethral meatus jutted an American or British flag. In this picture, he is wearing a pea jacket, and has a peanut vendor's box strapped to his shoulders. In the box are the candles. He somehow manages to look both proud and degenerate. Underneath the picture is his business card advertising "Ding-Dong Candles, Box 69, San Francisco, California 94701" with a copyright note and the statement "All rights reserved."

Sarah also forgives her mother. Like the "insanity plea," her mother is "crazy" and therefore should not be held accountable for her inertia. She did warm and loving things, but she could not stop Sarah's misery because she is "crazy." On the other hand, her step-father is a psychopath, whose intentions were always on the sur-face: to swindle and manipulate mother and children. Al's lack of subtlety is the primary reason that Sarah never considered forgiving him.

What effect did all of this have on Sarah? What kind of identity did she form and what did she think about herself? It is clear that many traditional boundaries were broken. From Sarah's experience, fathers are either absent or hostile, and overtly sexual. Mother does not come to the rescue. Stepbrother is hostile and overtly sexual. Parents do not work. And so on. Sarah's own sense of goodness was also challenged by a stepfather who was quick to label her a "liar, cheater, schemer, and whore." Sarah was ultimately domi-nated by a family which used coercion (sexual or otherwise) and withdrawal as a means of manipulating her feelings and behavior. Yet throughout her narrative, one always senses that Sarah has not given up. She is appalled, angry, depressed, and confused, but she keeps fighting to maintain her integrity. Daughters should not be raped by stepfathers. It is wrong, it hurts, and it is humiliating. Sarah does not lose sight of right and wrong, regardless of the abuse she receives. She wants a real father, she wants a strong mother, and so on. As will be seen later, although her parents were hideous role models, Sarah did obtain understanding elsewhere. Also, she absorbed enough of our cultural norms (through friends, TV, movies, and so on) to know what to expect from parents—and to know when parents have grossly deviated from that norm.

Despite her ability to maintain her integrity, Sarah paid a heavy price for this turmoil. It disrupted her friendships, her school work, and her relationships with authority figures.

> Needless to say . . . all of these problems led to diffi-culties with school. I had gone to public school until the fifth grade, but I had no rapport with any of the students.

We also moved around a lot so I didn't get to know that many kids. I guess I was a stranger for a long time. In fact, Karen and I were often the school scapegoats.

I also had a problem with social skills. Since my mother spent so much time attending to Al, she failed to teach us socially acceptable behavior. Things like . . . what is done, and what is not done. For me, it became a question of trial and error. And unfortunately, I had more than my share of errors.

Let me give you an example . . . First, I didn't know how to make friends. In the past, my friends were not very nice to me. It was just such a mess. I also didn't know how to dress nice, and in Bel Air, it wasn't appreciated. So I started getting a dreadful reputation. Besides my loneliness and sloppy dress, I also had a reputation for sex and drugs—even in elementary school and junior high school.

I never knew that drugs were such a big deal. I used to see Al buy marijuana and give it to his son. I also heard him say that cocaine was "the drug of the elite" or something stupid like that. As such, I felt that drugs must be pretty innocuous.

I was soon to find out, however, that when *I* used drugs (marijuana), all hell was to break loose. I was eleven, and Al was still around. He even kept me out of school when he found my marijuana. But this boy I went to school with came by, and I told him *why* I wasn't in school. He proceeded to tell the entire school, including the teachers.

As far as my sexual reputation is concerned, it had nothing to do with the incest. It's funny, I never thought of the incest as real sex . . . it was just something that was out there, but real sex was nice and a whole different thing. I remember that when I was nine I used to have lots of sexual fantasies. I also masturbated a lot. However, I didn't know that you were not supposed to masturbate in public. I made the mistake of masturbating during class. Of course, the boy sitting next to me was horrified. His face turned white and the teacher was looking at me. But the teacher didn't say anything, although I could feel her anxiety coming my way. That sort of told enough.

I felt like having sexual intercourse shortly after that. But I didn't know what to do about it. I had several older friends, so I could see them getting involved—but I felt completely excluded. Somehow I didn't fit in. Eventually (I was around eleven or twelve) I decided to lose my virginity, which I saw as a nuisance. But I also realized that no one was going to come up to an eleven-year-old and sweep her off her feet. So I started taking on a more assertive role in that area. I eventually found a willing stranger in a record store. He started talking to me, and I kept the conversation going. The conversation went on all day, and I went home with him. We fell into having sex.

I was scared. But it wasn't the sex that scared me . . . it was the situation—doing something that I had never done before. I liked the emotional part, but physically it was horrible. This person was very gentle, and I liked the attention I got. He made me feel special, and it was a strongly positive experience in that respect. But physically, it was horrible.

This guy was actually twenty-seven-years old, yet he didn't look it. He was also quiet. Although he knew that I was very young . . . the way I followed him around all day, he finally realized what I wanted. And he helpfully complied.

I felt that this experience was my initiation into womanhood. But I was also very scared. Fortunately, he didn't ejaculate inside me; he didn't ejaculate at all. So at least I wasn't worried about getting pregnant.

My mother never told me very much about sex—except the technicalities. I was very young and I had seen two dogs going at it. She told me something about being in heat and sperm cells. Later I remember seeing the word "fuck" written all over the place, and I asked her what it meant. She then told me, but I still couldn't figure out why people wrote it all over the walls. From my standpoint it didn't have such significance . . . you know, like social or cultural value.

When I asked her about love and sex, she told me that when she had sex with a man, she considered herself married at that point. That's about as far as love went. She eventually drew me some diagrams of a penis and ejaculate, and told me a little bit about menstruation and contraception. When I was six I found her diaphragm, and she explained what it was. That was all that I learned from my mother.

My father was very strict about contraception. He said "Never have sex unless you have a contraceptive. That's why you're here." So I learned that if my parents had used contraceptives, I wouldn't be here. I thought that was a strange way to explain it."

Although Sarah could distinguish between right and wrong parental behavior, she was less discriminating elsewhere. Was she unaware of the significance of masturbating at school, or was this her warning of the consequences of an incestuous family life? I believe it was the latter. It was her way of demonstrating to the world that she was a sexually abused child, i.e., that she had a distorted sense of sexual norms.

As I indicated earlier, Sarah does not use repression to expel her unpleasant memories. Instead, she uses "denial." Incest occurred, but "it wasn't sex." Thus, she is willing to note its occurrence, but she denies its significance. Excessive use of denial is often apparent in children who are repeatedly exposed to unpleasant, dangerous, and anxiety-provoking experiences. Since they have little power to deal with such situations, they deny their helplessness by either creating imaginary defenders, or by minimizing the potential harm. Sarah did the latter, and she maintains that stance to this day.

The absence of repression was helpful to Sarah because it allowed her to talk about her experiences. Thus, she could say that they did not bother her, or that they didn't matter, but by talking about them, she left herself open to other people's reactions. She could gain sympathy, support, notoriety, and so on because she was willing to talk. And even if she denied the extent of the abuse, she may have absorbed the concern and sympathy of others—at least at an unconscious level.

Sarah's assertiveness is also a significant factor in her ability to survive. When she wanted something tangible from her mother, she often managed to get it. The loss of virginity is another example of Sarah's assertiveness. It is unquestionably misdirected, but it is evidence of her ability to express a need (sexual intercourse), and direct her behavior to satisfy it. Eventually, this assertiveness and her ability to manipulate her environment served Sarah's desire to maintain her psychological stability and health.

Why would an eleven-year-old girl choose a twenty-seven-year-old man to have sex with? In Sarah's case, the answer is obvious. Since childhood, her sexual feelings and experience had been related to older men. Thus, the initiation of her own sexuality still bears resemblance to her incestuous past. Although she admits to finding sexual intercourse painful, she enjoyed the emotional warmth and intimacy. Children will often passively accept incestuous parents because it may be the only time they receive affection. This dynamic, however, is not unique to children of incestuous parents. Many people maintain sexual relationships in order to feel some warmth and physical intimacy (holding, touching, and so on).

Sarah's mother had very traditional views about sexuality and marriage. These views were also a target of Sarah's wrath. Her mother maintains that sex and marriage are identical. As the reader will see, Sarah will go to great lengths to prove otherwise. Sarah also rebels against her father's advice. She is nonchalant about contraception, and demonstrates a proclivity for getting pregnant. Again, it is evidence of her anger. Also, if Sarah is a good woman who has special meaning in this world, Sarah can create others in the same manner in which she was created, i.e., by contraceptive neglect.

Sarah uses sexuality for many reasons: to exert power, to establish independence, to express anger, and so on. Unfortunately, it is a double-edged sword. Her gains are closely matched with losses, which paradoxically, may also be her intention.

> When I was in junior high school I had my second sexual experience. I didn't know him very well, but I knew that I liked him enough to have sexual intercourse. I met him at a movie one night, and when he started making advances, I complied—and made some of my own. We went to a park and I started touching his penis, while he rubbed my clitoris. After we had intercourse, he just left. "Bye-bye, see you around" . . . that kind of thing. I wasn't used to this and I didn't know how to question him about it. With the first guy, I saw him several times afterward. But this was completely different. It was just in-and-out. That marked the close of having sex with people my own age.

> After that night, horrible things started to happen. This second guy told all of his friends—so they tried to gang rape me. I remember running away from them one day, running very fast, getting tackled, my sandals breaking, and having my pants ripped off. I think I fell down a hill, and several of them fell on top of me. When I saw somebody's crotch within grabbing distance, I squeezed real hard. Ironically, through the screaming, I could tell it was the boy I had screwed. His scream startled everyone else, so I had time to escape. I ran across Sunset Boulevard, with half my clothes ripped off, in broad daylight—while they were calling me a "PIG!"

> I transferred schools after this. I also started thinking about what it meant to be sexual. Basically, I felt that if

you liked someone, sex was a natural thing to do, especially if you loved the person. I had a little experience with Catholicism and catechism, which also influenced my ideas. I thought about one of the ten commandments: "Thou shalt not commit adultery." But I wasn't sure if this meant not having sex in general, or not having sex with someone's wife. Since my mother told me that it was important to have your own personal orientation to life, or your own conception of God, I interpreted things my own way. That meant that it was perfectly wonderful to have sex with someone outside of marriage, or with someone you liked. To me, this was completely acceptable.

I thought that certain things within the Catholic Church were absolutely stupid. They seemed contrary to what I experienced God to be. Baptism didn't make sense, and sexual prohibition didn't make sense. Of course, my father was always telling me, "Yes, sex is wonderful; go for free expression; go out there and sleep with people." He even sent pamphlets to me when I was twelve. But . . . when I finally starting sleeping around, my father had a fit. He would say, "What are you doing screwing around?", that kind of stuff. At this point I felt everything I did was wrong. It was a "no-win" situation.

You know my father really confused me. First, he never told me anything about love. It was completely sexual. And when he was in a "free expression" mood, he would tell me, "Go out, do what you want, sleep with whomever you want—just don't hurt anybody. And don't get pregnant." But he then didn't tell me anything about contraception, other than that I should go to a Free Clinic to get some. And as I said before, my mother also never mentioned love in the context of sex. Love, to her, was something that you looked up in the encyclopedia. She's not very good about expressing emotion.

There were times, during junior high school, when I had intercourse without using contraception. I think I wanted to get pregnant. Shake things up at home or something. I guess I felt I would get carted off to a girls' home . . . and this would be better for the moment. At that time, nothing really mattered . . . life didn't really matter. It's funny, although I knew about contraception, I felt that if I got pregnant, that would jar things up, and that was good. And if I didn't get pregnant, well, I thought that was good too. I guess I was convinced that I could handle the pregnancy—and be a better mother than my mother—even in junior high school. With all of our money, I knew that I could financially handle a child—it was the emotional side that I wasn't sure of.

I think that my parents would react very different to my getting pregnant at that age. My father would have been pissed off. I mean he wouldn't be upset like, "Oh God, look what you've done to your life" . . . it would be like, "You dummy." My mother, on the other hand, would probably have loved it. She would have not liked it in terms of my age, but she would have dealt with it. In fact, she'd probably raise it. It might have also gotten my stepfather out of the house real fast—because I wouldn't stay there with a child.

You know, I really didn't have sex that much between ages eleven and thirteen. To me, it was just a game—so I had a very playful attitude about it. It was also very exciting—and it gave me more respect with my older friends. (I think most of my friends were about seven years older.) It was my door to adulthood. My friends could now relate to me. I guess for some kids, it's smoking cigarettes which gives them status—for me it was intercourse.

Sex has another meaning for me. I remember being very lonely as a child—always wanting to be part of something. When I had sex, I finally found that excitement. It was very interesting, things were really happening. Although I confused some people, I started to have some close friends.

Of course, at first there were things I didn't like about sex. I was disgusted by oral sex because of the early exposure to it. My mother, however, told me this would change. This conversation came up because I had been reading a book where it was mentioned. I told my mother that I thought it was a violation. She started telling me that love isn't a violation . . . it's an expression . . . and oral sex is like any other expression of love. I said, "Okay, but it makes me sick."

Besides this early prohibition against oral genital sex (which I got over), I never made distinctions between sexual behaviors. I tended to make distinctions between boys . . . gentle versus hurting me. I was aware that some kids made distinctions according to "bases" (first, second, third, home), but I generally didn't, except perhaps when I was very young. At that time, I visualized intercourse as having someone trying to stick forks in me. I guess I got that from my experiences with my stepbrother.

I overcame my encounters with my stepfather and stepbrother by believing that they were the rotten apples, and that the rest of the world can't be that bad. My mother also gave me a very naive kind of home . . . "Everyone out there can be wonderful, loving, and gentle." If that's so, what about my stepfather? I used to think he was related to Hitler. For one thing, Al was anti-Semitic. Which was really great, given that my mother was sort of Jewish, and her parents were Jewish.

I have never been sure about my religion. I was raised Catholic, but I don't see myself as being Catholic. I haven't studied Judaism either. I didn't even think about being Jewish until I was twenty years old. I had this boyfriend who claimed that I must be Jewish. He had this proclivity to associate Jews with money, even though he realized that this was ridiculous.

When children are abused, they turn to fantasy. The world of illusion provides them with love, affection, and rewards. Unfortunately, this fantasy often becomes confused with the real world. In Sarah's case, she cannot distinguish between her fantasies about sexuality (love, kindness, sharing positive feelings) and the reality of sexuality. As a sexually abused child, Sarah created a world in which sexuality was a privileged form of communication (physical and emotional) between two diaphanous individuals. She projects this illusion upon her sexual partners, and as such, often fails to see their obvious limitations. Her second sexual partner is only one of such examples.

As I indicated in the introduction to this book, I am especially interested in the formation of Sarah's identity as evidenced in how she thinks about herself (i.e., *cognitive*). I'm also interested in how she constructs meaning out of her existence (i.e., *existentially*). The previous narrative provides considerable insight into both of these questions.

Religion serves many purposes, one of which is to prepare us for death. Religion consoles us in our grief, and fortifies us with promises of an afterlife (heaven, reincarnation, etc.). These assurances are important because we are painfully aware of our eventual demise. Although some of us may deny our fear of death, it is still the case that our prospects for the future are reflected in our mortality.

Most religions offer a solution, in terms of behaviors which will insure a happy afterlife. The ten commandments, sexual prohibitions, and so on are Western examples of behaviors which will foster the attainment of a satisfactory afterlife. Consequently, discussion of such topics is oftentimes a way of disguising a more basic issue, i.e., death. Sexual sin and damnation go hand in hand in many Western religions with ethical debates serving to articulate the specifics of that relationship (i.e., which "sins" are tolerable and which ones are not). In Sarah's case, I believe that her attempt to define and validate her sexual principles is an example of her feelings about death. In essence she is saying that her present life could be no worse than her afterlife, and as such, sexual prohibitions have no relevance for her. She is damned in the present, so why should she be concerned about being damned in the future? She will take what she can for now, and enjoy the pleasures that are available to her. As she indicates, sex also provides her with friendships, power, status, and so forth. So why should she follow "archaic" norms to prevent damnation when she has obviously been damned since birth?

Fortunately, Sarah presents another side of the argument. She is not damned, only the receiver of very bad luck. The "rotten apples" theory is testimony to this belief. Wonderful, gentle, and loving people do exist, and it is only misfortune that Sarah had encountered a predominance of rotten apples. "Persist and ye shall find" was a metaphor of considerable meaning to Sarah in her quest to discover people of merit. Consequently, throughout this narrative you will discover two Sarahs, one who behaves as if she has been damned since birth, and one who reasons that misfortune can be compensated for.

It should not be surprising to find that Sarah would vacillate between two opposing points of view. Her family life is full of contradictions. She has a Catholic mother, from a Jewish family; this mother marries an anti-Semite; her parents will discuss sex, but not love; her father encourages, and discourages sexual proliferation; and so on. These conditions have a created a young woman who does not know where she stands (on contraception, religion, sex, love, etc.), but is desperately trying to define herself—despite feeling that she wants to rebel against it all.

When I was about thirteen, I started to "expand" my horizons. This was the first time that I took a hallucinogenic drug. It was also the last time I took it . . . because I had such a horrible reaction to it. I saw devils coming out of the woods . . . and other horrible stuff. I was also very afraid . . . so I decided never to do that again. You know, to some people, I looked like a healthy, energetic, athletic kid, going to school and stuff . . . except that I had migraine headaches, asthma, muscle spasms, and so on. My mother's theory was that I had internalized all these problems into my body. To her . . . that is all that it was.

The drug that I took was peyote, soaked in Coca-Cola. When I first took it, I didn't experience any sickness, so I went to school. (It was an algebra class I was taking during the summer.) But I was having trouble riding my bicycle. Also, I felt these problems in my neck, and my arms and legs . . . like my arteries and veins were shifting. I could feel the blood.

After this drug experience, I decided to get serious. I was still interested in sex, but I wanted to become involved in school . . . and then go into medicine. But it was difficult studying at my mother's home. This was my biggest challenge between the ages of thirteen and fourteen. I mean, dogs were always barking—or even jumping through plate glass windows. Which, by the way, my mother didn't get fixed, so that the Santa Ana winds would blow through, plus stray dogs and cats.

We were living in Malibu at the time. So when I had to study, I would go on the beach at night, near one of the overhead lights. I actually did very well in school, even with all of these things against me. But it was also at this time that I started losing my ability to cope. It first manifested itself as depression. I was working very hard in school—much harder than I needed to, but my home was falling apart. My stepbrother had moved back in, and brought all of these friends who were on SSI. SSI is money you get from the government if you are legally insane. Everyone was on drugs all of the time, carrying on like "elitist pre-war decadents." You know, like the movie

Cabaret. (By the way, my stepbrother eventually became a homosexual.)

There were lots of crazy parties too. My mother wasn't around much, so these transvestites would come over, acting like *Divine* in *Pink Flamingos*. It was very colorful. When they didn't party, they took drugs and read books. They never worked. The most constructive thing they ever did was to go to the beach to get a suntan.

All of my stepbrother's friends had a strange attitude. It was "Everything is fucked." "Get all you can." There was nothing enlightened about them. Of course, I've seen some of these people recently—they're all married and very conservative. But then, they were "crazy."

Besides disrupting my school life, they were getting Karen involved in their act. Karen was thirteen, and she fell in love with one of my stepbrother's friends. He was the first person she ever slept with. I could have killed him. He was so obnoxious—so awful. After they split up—about six months later—she had her first psychotic experience. Hearing voices, and all of those kinds of things. She was hospitalized at this time.

It was very strange when Karen first went through this. There were a lot of people around: my stepbrother and his friends, her best friend who was living with us, and so on. It was very chaotic. But this man didn't care that she was too young for him; he was twenty-eight, and such a snob. Before this man, Karen was very passive and subdued. After him, she was crazy. He didn't really want her—he wanted her best friend . . . Heather. It just destroyed Karen emotionally. She may have looked seventeen, but psychologically she was eleven. Even today, I would say that psychologically she is only about thirteen.

Of course, Karen had her problems before this guy. She was always kind of flaky. She had problems making friends—and had this strange legacy in Malibu. She also never talked if something bothered her. She just wouldn't say anything. I've only recently realized how much hatred she had . . . toward my mother. But she would just retire into herself.

Our environment had a lot to do with Karen's problems. I don't think she had incest with Al, but we both seemed to have everything smashed into our faces. And my mother . . . sometimes she would be there. Other times not. She wouldn't make a conscious effort to understand things.

I also hated my mother for this. I mean . . . all the things that happened to me, before I was eleven. I had been done a great injustice, and I couldn't get rid of this feeling. This anger, I could talk about it—but it wouldn't relieve anything. I felt like it was an endless pit. I would never be able to purge myself of this hatred. I just seemed to be going around and around.

Karen felt these things too, but she would never express it. Today, she claims that she was the only one who suffered . . . that only she was singled out . . . beaten . . . yelled at . . . humiliated. She *was* very humiliated. For instance, Karen liked to draw, and she had these pastels. But she only drew beautiful things. Well . . . one day, there were these pastel drawings on the garage. They didn't look like Karen's. They looked like Al's. But Al claimed Karen did it. The next thing I remember is that Al asked me for my favorite color. So I picked it out. He then said, "Draw on your sister! Draw on her face! Just draw on it!" Of course, I became paralyzed. So he took the pastel and started drawing on her, just all over her. Then he told her that she had to leave it on all day. It was her "punishment." I remember trying to make Karen feel better by telling her she looked like a beautiful peacock.

Karen never tried to wash this stuff off. I guess she was afraid of Al's wrath. But she remembers every detail of this, even today. Oftentimes, she tries to minimize what happened to me, by recalling experiences like these.

When Karen had this first psychotic episode, she was thirteen. She was acting very . . . very strange. Her eyes were all dilated . . . her skin was fiery, and she was hearing voices. I think the voices were saying wonderful things . . . but she was also crying . . . very spaced out.

Karen was put in the hospital for two weeks. I think it was USC hospital. But two weeks turned into months, and the whole thing turned into a big fiasco. She was diagnosed as schizophrenic. I think the psychologist was a charlatan. He thought it was a behavioral problem which he could "shape" out of her. I mean he'd hit her . . . I could kill him. He was this huge guy, but he finally referred her elsewhere. But God . . . what an idiot . . . she came out of the second place more freaked out than ever. She was now paranoid on top of everything else . . . with that system of "rewards and punishments." What a mess! It took her a long time to get back to a reasonable state. But the doctors wanted her institutionalized again. They didn't like the "unwholesome" environment at home. They also wouldn't let Karen see my father, so he kept staging plans to break her out of the hospital. My mother just put all the responsibility into the "man's" hand.

When Karen was in the hospital she didn't say very much. She was very catatonic. I think a lot of scary things happened to her when she had to face the emotional side of adolescence. That is, the intensity of it, plus the biological things like puberty.

Karen never had a chance. The family turmoil and abuse would ultimately create psychosis in most children—and certainly at least one child per family would suffer. In this family, that role fell to Karen. She was the patient, the overt symbol of a disturbed and traumatized upbringing. She differed from Sarah in at least two meaningful ways. First, Sarah was the oldest, and as such, was often thrust into the role of caretaker. Sarah had to be strong, and was reinforced for being strong by her passive mother, her absent father, and her dependent sister. Secondly, Sarah was an extrovert. Although she lacked social skills, she had a strong need to communicate—which often included talking about her childhood. As I indicated earlier, while Sarah may have denied the significance of much of the turmoil, her ability to talk about this topic was likely to have garnered support and sympathy from others.

Karen, on the other hand, was a withdrawn and passive little girl. In her photographs she appears vacant and lost. Her small face is engulfed by a thick mass of long brown hair—which also accentuates her excess weight. As Sarah indicated, Karen looks more like her mother, whereas Sarah's blond hair and light complexion is closer to her father's characteristics.

Karen undoubtedly suffered the abuse and humiliation of incest, plus the demented malice of her stepfather. Moreover, her passive mother offered no relief from this turmoil. It is interesting to note that Sarah can express her own anger at her mother when the subject of Karen is brought up. I believe that this reflects two feelings. First, it is a genuine hostility toward her mother. Secondly, however, I believe that Sarah feels guilty (and responsible) about Karen. Sarah survived but Karen did not—and I believe that Sarah questions whether she could have done more. Sarah was thrust into the role of parent (even as early as eight years old), and Karen is an obvious failure. Sarah's anger at her mother and Karen's psychologist is a veiled criticism of herself, and of her parents. Sarah also wanted to deny the magnitude of Karen's psychosis, as her comment "I think the voices were saying wonderful things" reveals, because Sarah did not want to acknowledge her own failure as a caretaker. Of course, there is no reason that Sarah should feel this way—except that her parents manipulated her into this role.

Unfortunately, the turmoil does not end here. Sarah's stepbrother and his entourage are more fuel for the fire. Karen's relationship with a twenty-eight-year-old man is not surprising, given her incestuous past. This man, regardless of his own stability, undoubtedly gave the appearance of providing love, support, and affection to Karen. He became her savior—because she was desper-

I asked Gayle Partlow, an artist who resides in Los Angeles, to read this book. When she was finished, I asked Gayle to draw pictures of Sarah and Karen, based solely upon the feelings created by this book. The cover drawing of Sarah and this one of Karen are the results.

ately in need of saving. When he left, however, Karen lost both her savior and her belief that she could be saved, thereby succumbing into psychosis.

While all of this hospital stuff was going on for Karen, I was living with my boyfriend in my mother's house. His name was John, and I met him in my mother's kitchen. It was not unusual for me to come home from school and see someone in the house I'd never seen before. On this day, when I came home, there was this guy in the kitchen. No one seemed to know how he got there. Later, I learned that he was the brother of a friend of Karen's. This friend was going to take LSD for the first time, and she wanted to have John around. Just to make sure that she wouldn't have any problems.

John and I started talking in the kitchen. He was the most refreshing personality I had met in years. And we just kept talking. In fact, we spent the whole night talking. He then stayed over, which didn't delight my mother. I guess she was afraid of our emotional connection. There were certainly enough other people hanging around, most of them having sex . . . but with John, there was something different.

(John wouldn't have intercourse with me until I got birth control. We had oral sex, but we didn't have intercourse. And with him, the oral sex was great.) This was a difficult time for my mother. When John was with me, she would want me to have the door open a little . . . "just in case." *Yeah!* . . . just in case Al came home so that he could make a scene. Although the divorce was through, Al was still antagonizing us. My mother went to the police, but all they did was to tell Al to go home. And then later that night, he would sneak over, put his fist through the windows, yell and scream—and then disappear. And, of course, when the police would finally come back, he would be gone.

Eventually, my mother accepted John living with me. She wasn't happy with it, but to appease her, I'd leave the door open—but we would still have sex. She would walk in the room, and then turn away. After a while, she shut the door.

The neighborhood kids would also walk in the room while we were having sex. I remember one time, John was going down on me and didn't stop. He didn't care about the children. However he eventually got up and kicked them out. The next day I got a deadbolt.

After about a month of living in my mother's house, John and I moved into the master bedroom. My mother stayed in one of the smaller rooms. It was a very refreshing time for John and I . . . a *real* "love affair." It wasn't just sleeping with people, but reciprocal emotional contact. I was very fond of him, and it was reciprocated. It was a wonderful time in my life.

I was in love with John. But I was also in love with being in love. It was that kind of a special relationship. And John loved me. We're still good friends. John, by the way, helped me become totally orgasmic. I was orgasmic before him, but I perfected it while we were together. I think we had sex three times a day. You know, "young at heart."

John and I were very sexually experimental. He used to masturbate so that I could listen to his heartbeat. We'd do strange things like that. It was all very "trial and error." But before him, there didn't seem to be much "fun" in sex. I can remember this short affair I had several months before meeting John. I was depressed and I met this guy, Jake, at a drunken party. We ended up in bed. It was exciting because he was very attractive. But he wouldn't talk to me, and I didn't know how to talk to him. When this affair ended, he said, "I'm leaving tomorrow morning for Washington." (He was a young lawyer, twenty-five years old, and I was fourteen or fifteen.) "Drop by, or give a call, if you're ever in town." I mean it wasn't like "I care for you." It was sort of a common courtesy, being polite. In fact, I doubt that he wanted me to drop by.

This short affair depressed me. There wasn't anything specific about it, it was just everything felt like shit. So I started getting more involved in school. But that didn't work. I would just go home, sit on my bed, and do nothing. And then I had trouble going to class . . . I was falling apart. I'd just start crying, or feeling dizzy. I did that for a while, and my teachers and friends thought that I needed a break. I guess I looked overworked. Fortunately, I was going to a private school, so I could take an unscheduled vacation—for about a month and a half.

I went to stay with my dad in San Francisco. He wasn't around very much; he had this lovely Chinese girlfriend. I also lived out in the streets . . . which was ridiculous . . . sleeping with bums on the sidewalks.

Karen's friend Heather also came up and stayed with me for a while. We would just walk the streets, talking to people, sort of learning the rules. One rule we learned was that you don't say you don't have a place to stay. That was interpreted as meaning that you were looking for someone to screw. Of course, I did go to bed with someone, but Heather didn't. She sort of had an aggrandized virginity. Eventually, we were both very disappointed. Although we tried to befriend the street people by taking them to restaurants, we were still very lonely. So we both went back to school.

I guess there was one other brief affair before I met John. I was hitchhiking and this guy in a truck stopped to pick me up. We talked . . . and then we screwed. But there was no warmth . . . no eye contact. It was like I wasn't there. Something about this experience made me seriously consider being a homosexual.

Actually . . . I forgot . . . there were a number of other one-night stands before I met John. I kept screwing different guys, each time hoping it would be different . . . but it wasn't. I even tried different circumstances and different kinds of people . . . but it was the pits. I guess I thought about homosexuality because my girlfriends were much warmer to me.

Fortunately, after all of these escapades, I met John. As I mentioned before, we got along very well. At some point, however, he decided that our relationship should be "open." It seemed kind of reasonable to me, in that I was so young (fifteen), and didn't need to be tied to one person for life. What I didn't know was that it meant John was going to screw my best girlfriend.

I guess I took the "open relationship" very theoretically. I was very happy so I didn't look for anyone else. Then one night I came home and John told me that he screwed my best friend. It was the pits . . . but I guess I didn't take it too bad. I took a long walk. I went through my pain, my hurt, my anger, and all those things. I also decided not to sleep with him for about a month because my girlfriend had every venereal disease in the book. I told him, "Next time, be a little more selective." As for my friend, I fought with her . . . which kind of neutralized things. She was so pathetic.

Shortly after this episode another girlfriend of mine wanted to have a *ménage à trois* with John and I. She initiated this while John and I were visiting her. I think John also wanted to have sex with her. As we started to have sex, it became clear that I was being left out. It was like this situation is going on in front of me, and "of course, we want you to be there." But it was obvious to me that I wasn't wanted.

This all started when this girlfriend began com-
menting about my hair . . . touching my clothes. Then
she took off her clothes . . . and started touching me. It
was like . . . ugh . . . being touched by someone who
doesn't want to touch you. I guess I was upset because
she didn't care about me. She was only doing it to get at
John. It had nothing to do with me. Then she started
kissing John, and then me . . . Ugh. I guess I kissed her
until it was obvious that I wasn't wanted, so I got up and
left the room. I remember thinking "Okay, this can be
handled." But it hurt me incredibly. I thought it would be
all right as long as John loved me . . . but it wasn't.

I went back to her room about an hour later, but they
were still at it, so I went home. But it turned out to be a
many-times thing . . . often while I was in the same
room. The three of us would be watching T.V., and all of
a sudden, she'd be stroking him and kissing him, you
know. Then I'd get up and leave.

I finally started seeing someone else. Also, John's
mother was becoming increasingly uncomfortable with
his living with me. He was only seventeen, and I guess
she wanted him around the house. His father had recently died.

The guy I started seeing lived in Hollywood. He was a
publicity manager for Columbia records and the Rolling
Stones. He was a very nice man . . . a real sweetie pie.
Actually, he was the man who convinced me to start therapy. I didn't want to go to therapy because my mother
had been in therapy before . . . and I'd seen how much
"good" it did for her. But, I was feeling bad over John . . .
so I decided to give it a try. However, I also kept seeing
the publicity manager. I guess this finally affected John in
a strange way. John would give me a ride to see this guy,
and I would tell John, "Well, I'm not going to come home
tonight." But John would say, "Well, I'll sit and wait in
the car." Sometimes it'd be all night, and John would wait

all night. John claimed he was waiting for both of us. He said that it was wrong for him to make demands on me, and since I wasn't old enough to drive, he was going to stick by his philosophy. Actually, I think it was upsetting him.

Consciously, I don't think that I was seeing this man to get back at John. John had already taken less interest in me sexually, saying that he found other bodies more exciting. Also, he was doing other shitty kinds of things. I remember that I took a job at a Mexican restaurant (my first and only real job), to save enough money to buy him a tennis racket for his birthday. He immediately sold the racket, claiming that he decided against taking tennis lessons. I guess, given these kinds of circumstances, I just wanted to be with someone else.

Of course, I didn't throw John out. I just couldn't understand why he was treating me badly. It didn't make any sense to me. I guess I was just being passive about it. I think part of my problem is that I had such a "wonderful" model in my mother . . . who could have her head smashed in, and still stay with my stepfather. You know . . . I remember once . . . Al took her head and just smashed it like a basketball against the kitchen sink. And when my mother went to call the police, he ripped the phone off the wall and started to strangle her. I mean her mind has never been the same since. A lot of things don't pull together for her. I also remember another time when Al smashed her in the face, leaving a whole side of her face black and blue. My feelings for my mother were so astounding . . . I couldn't believe that it was happening . . . I couldn't believe that he could do that.

I guess my feelings for John and my girlfriend were like: "I couldn't believe that they could do that to me." When John and I finally split up, he started calling me a vicious whore. I didn't deserve that. Anyway . . . John moved back with his mother. I was sixteen at that time

. . . and I also decided to move out. My mother's house
was so overrun by strange people that I needed to be on
my own. Of course, John wanted to live with me again . .
. but I said, "No, forget it!" It was so hard . . . so difficult.
And I couldn't tell if I had become hardened.

It is disheartening to watch a child stumble. It is even more disturbing when the fall seems inevitable. And for Sarah, it will take
all of her strength to pick herself up again, and again, until she is
on a stable course. Unfortunately, it is a long way off. That "wonderful" mother is not only a poor model, but a pathetic person. It
will be difficult for Sarah to establish a self-fulfilling relationship because her feelings are so oblique. She needs a strong, caring man,
but she is very angry at men (father, stepfather, etc.); she wants a
compassionate, stable woman, but she is very angry at women
(mother); she gets satisfaction out of taking care of people, but she
also wants them to take care of her; she needs to feel wanted, but
she also wants to rebel; and so on. Consequently, her relationships
manifest a bipolar tendency, vacillating between intimacy and
aloofness.

As I have stated throughout this book, Sarah's need to communicate is an essential ingredient to her ultimate survival. She met
John, in her mother's kitchen, and talked all night long. Her talking
facilitates understanding, sympathy, compassion, and accep-
tance—feelings which are often non-existent in her family life. Regardless of the outcome of her relationships, she is able to create
rapport through her need to communicate.

Sarah's narrative is further testimony to the disintegration of a
family. The house was a menagerie. The children were not safe,
and they were sexually abused. The mother was physically abused.
Consequently, other standards were also disintegrating. The
mother moved out of the master bedroom because of pressure from
her fifteen-year-old daughter. Sexual standards (i.e., door ajar)
were stated, but were ignored by both daughter *and* mother. The
boundaries of Sarah's relationship with John were never clearly re-

solved. Sarah entertained homosexuality because her relationships with men were routinely unsatisfactory. Sarah also contributed to the futility of her relationships by initiating random sexual encounters (hitchhiking, etc.) which could only increase her feelings of rejection. And in some ways, to spite her stepfather, she was fulfilling his stereotypic prophecy, i.e., being the "slut" or "whore." Unfortunately, her anger was misdirected because it only brought her pain, and did not hurt him.

Throughout the course of this narrative you will read many examples of Sarah's naiveté. She is not that naive, however. The naiveté is in the service of her major defense mechanism, denial. She covered up the abusive reality of her family life with denial, and in its place she created a fantasy version. As I indicated earlier, her fantasy version of sexual relations is a poor match for the reality of her sexual encounters. The *ménage à trois* is just one more example. Unfortunately, her denial also extends to a variety of other circumstances, including the street people of San Francisco. In fact, many of her problems are a result of denying the danger or severity of her circumstances.

> Moving out of my mother's house was not that easy. When I first asked her, she said no . . . she wouldn't like it. I told her that I wasn't sure that I would like it either, but I thought it might be a good thing. In my mind, it was a "trial separation."
>
> I moved to Venice (California), near the old post office. It was a very dirty location, with a lot of traffic. The only entertaining aspect of this apartment was that it was also near the police station. I could watch the police come and go.
>
> I paid for the apartment with money I got from my father. My father had stopped paying child support because Al used to steal it. So I took my "share" directly from my father. I also had a car. My grandparents gave

me a new Saab for my sixteenth birthday. My grandparents also gave me a monthly allowance.

This apartment was a real change for me, although I didn't spend much time there. I tended to spend most of my time on the streets of Venice. I also didn't bring many people back to my apartment. The few that did come back either stole things from me or broke things. I remember I had this banjo player friend, in his thirties, who used to come knocking at my door at 3 AM. He would make so much noise that I would let him in . . . so as not to disturb the neighbors. But he would just steal things from me.

When I lived in Venice, I didn't go to high school. I just dropped out. I was having enough emotional problems that I decided to wipe the slate clean and just stay out of school for the year. I don't know what I did with all of my time . . . except turning tricks.

I got into the prostitution thing when I met a prostitute at a party. Her boyfriend was also there. She was telling me how you approach people . . . just talking very diplomatically, like "Are you interested in spending the night with me?" She was working at the big resort hotels in Mexico. I guess she was very attractive to the Mexicans because she was a pretty blond woman. She said she made $25,000 in three months. Before she went to Mexico, she worked the streets of Los Angeles.

I thought that this was very fascinating . . . but I also thought that I couldn't do it. Thus, it was a challenge, and also something very different. I have a strong taste for doing something different . . . trying anything once. I was also in awe of this woman . . . I couldn't believe that you could just go up to someone and present yourself that way.

Being a prostitute seemed very interesting to me. At that party, I also met someone who said that he could help me get jobs . . . and protection. This "pimp," his name was Chico, had a fascination with me . . . he asked me if I would be his girlfriend. But I couldn't stand him. I think he had one other woman.

Chico got me one job. I went to this older man's house somewhere in the Hollywood Hills. The older man wanted to watch Chico and I have sex. I think the older guy couldn't get an erection . . . so he was more interested in either watching sex, or having oral sex with a woman. I think it was also an aesthetic thing on the older guy's part . . . it was almost like he wanted to watch you dance or something. Which would have been okay, but I couldn't stand Chico.

You know Chico was so obnoxious . . . so ridiculous. He thought he was such a big deal because he was educated in Europe. I remember one time he had this little get-together in Beverly Hills. There was a swimming pool there. Chico thought that it would be real avant-garde to shit in a Beverly Hills swimming pool. He would do things like that.

I don't think I had intercourse with Chico that night. I don't remember what we did. I just hated being around him. The older man was very nice. Afterwards, we had a long talk. He told me that he pays women to be his escorts. I guess he had a lot of money, and liked to have young women go with him to concerts or the theater. After these women worked as his "escorts," he would help them with their other careers, like acting, school, or paying for portfolios.

Chico also set up a phone service for me. But out of the goodness of my heart (I was so generous), I gave many of my clients to a friend. I did this because I couldn't stand Chico.

Of course, I took some clients. One young man had just won money at the race track. He had never been with a prostitute before. My girlfriend and I both went over to his house. He was very embarrassed by the whole thing.

I was scared. In some respects, I was scared for my life. But I never had any real problems while I was a prostitute, yet I was still afraid of getting arrested. It would probably kill my grandparents. My mother found out about this . . . but not until after I stopped being a prostitute. I think a friend of mine told her. At first, she didn't believe it.

When I try to understand why I did this . . . I think part of it had to do with my strong curiosity . . . I also never felt guilty . . . ashamed . . . or depressed about it. I didn't have any of these feelings . . . until just recently. I think being a prostitute was also one way of getting attention. People were very appreciative of me. In thinking back, the only time I got positive attention from my stepfather was after he had sex with me. I've often wondered if that was the connection. I mean it could be, but I don't know. In general, sex was a way to get the attention that I had difficulty getting otherwise. I also had a lot of power as a prostitute . . . but I didn't realize this until it was over.

I had two bad experiences while turning tricks. One wasn't even a trick of mine . . . but my friend said that he was too fat for her, so this trick said he wanted to have sex with me. He was so rude . . . but I decided to go through with it. He started to take off his clothes and I took off mine. He told me that he liked my body . . . but it was in such a vulgar, hard way. He then got on top of me, and I spread my legs. It felt very mechanical, and was over within twenty seconds.

It was strange . . . while it was going on, I was trying to figure out why he was so rude. I didn't really think about him being "on top of me." It wasn't very physical, and I wasn't really there. Actually, I was rather surprised. He wasn't on me long enough for me to think, "Oh, this awful person is on top of me!" I was shocked about how fast he came. He entered me and ejaculated. It was the fastest thing I'd ever seen.

In many ways, I don't think that I was even aware that he ejaculated. It just didn't register . . . except that it was very bizarre. When this guy was done . . . he said that he wasn't going to pay me. He owed me $100, which was my rate. We got into a big fight . . . and he finally gave it to me. Chico didn't help at all. When I got the money . . . I gave it to my girlfriend, who was supposed to screw him in the first place. I felt sorry for her, and she needed the money for a trip we were going to take to New York. This woman (whose name was Patti) was also my lover.

Patti and I became sexual when we worked as prostitutes. The two of us were having sex with one man. At one point, I decided to to make my feelings clear, so I pushed the guy aside and went down on Patti. It was very interesting. It was the first time I had sex with a woman. I got so involved that I forgot that the guy was there. But later . . . I came to realize that Patti didn't like it, she was just acting for the guy. I guess this disturbed me. I really wanted a relationship with her. But she didn't respond . . . she never responded. It was a very frustrating affair.

Of course, I never said to Patti that I wanted a relationship with her. Talking about it would have been very bizarre. I felt better about going down on her as a symbol of my intentions . . . somehow it was more expressive. I was also afraid of being rejected . . . and I guess I felt that if I excited her, it would temporarily offset the rejection. So I would first kiss her, then explore her, and then go down on her. But she gave me no eye contact . . . no sign that she cared. It was all for the guy. We each collected our $75.00.

I still tried to carry on a relationship with Patti. But it was like I was there and she wasn't. I guess she found it amusing. Of course, I never thought that it was wrong for

me to be sexual with another woman. I felt that if you
have a need, then you should express it. John and I used
to talk about this. He tried a homosexual affair once. He
claimed the man was really wonderful, but he was sure
that he didn't want to be a homosexual.

I was hurt by Patti. She was just tolerating me. When
she was horny, she didn't want to sleep with me . . . she
wanted to sleep with a man. I didn't think that she didn't
like me . . . only that she didn't want to have sex with
me. She was a bit strange anyway. She stole from her parents, stole from me. She would do things that you would
never expect a friend to do. She is a heroin addict now
. . . as well as a prostitute.

I never got into heroin. I have this thing about nee-
dles. I faint at a blood test. I also remember seeing nee-
dles in an Andy Warhol film . . . I felt so sick that I almost
didn't make it to the bathroom. So I never did anything
that involved a needle. I guess I could have snorted heroin . . . but no one offered it to me.

After I got rid of Chico, I decided to do it on my own.
I would go into hotel lobbies and just sit down. I guess I
looked like a sixteen-year-old girl from a wealthy family,
so I was never told to leave. But older men were always
approaching me. I remember this one guy, he must have
said "Hi" two hundred times. Finally, he invited me to
dinner, but I didn't tell him right away that I was a prostitute. I guess I was curious . . . and I also wanted to limit
myself to one trick that night.

When this guy finally asked me to go to his hotel
room, I then told him I was a prostitute. He said okay,
and asked me how much I wanted. So I told him $100.
Of course, with inflation today, I would have probably
charged him more. I actually enjoyed sex with him, until
he started calling me his mother. He actually called me
"mom." I mean this guy was gigantic, about 6'7"
and forty years old. He owned a chain of health spas.

It was strange to be called mom when I was only six-teen years old. Sometimes . . . people would think I was fourteen. At other times twenty-three. It all depended on my frame of mind. But this guy knew I was a prostitute. He was a little surprised by it, but he didn't seem to mind. Later that evening he told me he wanted me for another evening. In fact, he wanted me to live with him at his ranch in Oregon. I had so many proposals you wouldn't believe it.

You know, I really believed that this guy was single. I guess some of my other friends had been with him . . . and they also said he was single. But he didn't talk very much. He just stared into my eyes and said, "Hi." And when we had sex, we just walked all over the place. I was hip level, about four feet off the ground, and he would walk around while we were having intercourse.

I also felt that this guy was trying to make emotional contact with me, but he didn't know how. He kept want-ing me to stay with him, so I stayed a couple of days. When we would walk by a store, he would want to buy me something. He bought me a lot of clothes, but when I said goodbye, I left the clothes with him.

You know, in some ways I was a horrible prostitute. First, I hated shopping. It was very uncomfortable for me. This guy would be saying, "Try this on," "Put that on" . . . but I would just want to leave. The one thing that I *wasn't* uncomfortable about doing was having sex.

I finally left this guy when he became overbearing. He kept asking me to come live with him. He also wanted to pay for my rent and everything else, which started to scare me. When I said goodbye, I didn't charge him . . . I just wanted to get out. I think I told him that I had some business to attend to, but that I would be back. I was so smart . . . I never gave anyone my address or phone number . . . so he couldn't trace me. He was just getting too emotional.

After about a week, I went back to that hotel. It is really a beautiful building. But the next guy who came up to me knew that I was a prostitute. There was a good reason why he knew; he owned a large prostitution ring in New York. He started giving me all these do's and don'ts of prostitution. It was amazing; I wished I had a tape recorder; he talked so fast. I guess my biggest problem was that I didn't have a very businesslike attitude. For me it was just curiosity. To him it was business. He also told me about all the legal constraints . . . undercover detectives and so on. He told me, "Don't take off the first piece of clothing." This was a whole dimension that I wasn't aware of.

Eventually, this guy asked me if I would go to Toronto. He knew this man who was looking for a full-time mistress. I thought it might be interesting. I had never been to Canada. I also thought that it might be interesting to meet this person. But I didn't go. The only thing that stopped me was my grandparents. I was afraid that it would kill them if I went away. I guess I felt that it was worse to leave the city than to stay in Los Angeles to be a prostitute. That is, my grandparents didn't inquire into my affairs as long as I was in Los Angeles. But if I went somewhere else, they probably would have kept tabs on me. My grandparents were the only stable influence that I had in my life . . . My mother was so flaky. And it wasn't like they were authority figures . . . but I just didn't want to hurt them.

I never went to the same hotel more than five or six times. I was afraid of getting recognized. I also tried to change the way I looked. This was done to conceal my identity in case I ran into my grandparents' friends. Many of their friends would stay in these ritzy hotels. I guess I thought that their friends would wonder, "What the hell are you doing in the lobby?" God forbid any of their friends "calling" on me.

Most of the people I met in these hotel lobbies were very superficial. Conventioneers. The only one who stands out is that 6'7" guy. I used to charge each of these people something different. Sometimes . . . I would have sex with someone for about a half an hour and charge him $100.00. Another time I would spend the whole evening . . . going out to dinner, doing a whole social thing . . . and charge less or the same amount. It just depended. Sometimes I didn't even charge at all. Those that I didn't charge were usually men that I had some rapport with . . . or felt sorry for. I remember this little old Jewish man . . . when I told him that I wasn't going to charge him, he was ecstatic. It was so cute.

I think that I had a sincere curiosity about all of the people that I was with. To me, sex couldn't be mechanical. I'd seen some French movies where prostitutes didn't even take their clothes off. They would just lift up their dresses . . . no kissing, no stuff like that. To me, sex was very playful. I might start by taking off my customer's clothing . . . talking to them . . . touching them. I often took baths with them. Not the ones that I didn't like . . . but for the ones that I did like, I made it a whole evening. We would talk, have intercourse, watch T.V., or go out.

There was this other man who wanted to be my girlfriend . . . (laughs) . . . I mean he wanted to be my boyfriend. After I had seen him a few times professionally, he wanted to see me on a regular, boyfriend-girlfriend basis. I think he hired a private detective to get my address and phone number. But I didn't see him after that.

Between the ages of fifteen and seventeen, I was always sexually excited. But I didn't try to turn as many tricks as I could. I guess I wanted to enjoy my work. If you have a job, it's nice to try and find some redeeming qualities in what you do. What I liked best about being a prostitute was the adventure. The diversity of people. It was so strange, seeing all of these different people, business men, Marina Del Rey swingers . . . it was like being part of these different worlds.

Like many of her previous experiences, prostitution was a mixed bag. It provided her with attention, instant friendships, appreciation, power, and an identity. Sarah was now a prostitute. On the other hand, it was emotionally void, it was potentially dangerous, it would hurt her grandparents, and it involved contact with organized crime. Sarah's characteristic response to all of this was to acknowledge the pros and cons, but to deny their significance. Instead, it was an "adventure," and a nice way to meet a "diversity of people." When it was particularly difficult, as with the "rude fat man," she denied all of her emotions (i.e., sex, disgust, shame, etc.), and proceeded to clinically analyze how long it took him to ejaculate. She concludes, "In many ways, I don't think that I was even aware that he ejaculated. It just didn't register." As seen earlier, many of Sarah's sexual experiences "just didn't register." Sarah also mentions that she felt no guilt, shame, or depression then, but does now. As her psychological stability increases, her reliance on denial diminishes.

Why did Sarah have sex with the "rude fat man"? He was not her client to begin with, and certainly not her responsibility. But Sarah is determined to be a "friend in need," because for much of her life, no friend existed. And how much better to be a savior for Patti even it if meant having sex with a disgusting, angry, and obese man. Besides, Sarah felt very attracted to Patti, and what better way to establish one's allegiance. When this failed, Sarah tried a more direct approach, sexual contact with Patti. But like that country and western song, "I've been looking for love in all the wrong places," Sarah could not have picked a less likely target for emotional intimacy. In her photographs, Patti looks like a drugged, sex queen from an Andy Warhol movie. Resplendent in her tiger-patterned dress, left open to expose her breasts and crotch, Patti feigns all the airs of an exhausted movie star. In a series of other photographs, she appears more manic, in a red silk dress that accentuates her height and large frame. And as Sarah has indicated, the passage of time has not been kind to Patti. She is still a prostitute, but now also a heroin addict.

Why would Sarah want to become involved with Patti, especially when Patti ignored her advances, stole from her, and so on? For that matter, why did Sarah maintain contact with all the "friends" who stole from her, or with Chico, whom she detested from the beginning? First of all, Sarah badly needed contact with people, and this was probably apparent to all those who met her. Also, her gentle, caring, "I can help you" look probably made her an easy target. Consequently, people were eager to take everything she had. But as I have mentioned before, Sarah was determined to be a savior. So what if people abused her, isn't that the fate of all saints? Her prostitution was also motivated by a similar objective. She would provide sex to the downtrodden, the unattractive, or socially unsophisticated. Money was inconsequential. She had plenty and was soon to inherit more. This circumstance also gave her considerable freedom because she could pick and choose at will. Thus, she was a bad prostitute/businesswoman, but this concern was secondary to the psychological motives for her behavior.

Like most self-destructive forms of behavior, prostitution creates more problems than anticipated. It may have satisfied Sarah's curiosity and need for excitement, but it certainly exacerbated her fears of rejection. While she was ultimately in control of her "tricks," the prostitution experience would never endear her to those she loved (or would love). And the most significant people at *that* time were her grandparents (on her mother's side). Her grandmother and grandfather provided her with love, support, understanding, and stability. They were there for Sarah, they did not abuse her (sexually or otherwise), and they treated her with uniform kindness. Unfortunately, while her grandparents were a key to Sarah's psychological survival, they were not a barrier to the abuse she received from the rest of the family. Consequently, Sarah had strong needs to rebel and retaliate, despite her affection and concern for her grandparents. The following dream (from Sarah's diary) is evidence of the significance of her grandmother's stabilizing influence:

Last night I dreamt that I was at this house and I was a part of a family that lived there. There were these two men in it too. This dream is very vague but the two men had this method of turning people into zombies who didn't have a will of their own but did what the two men said. They did this to me. They stuck this long needle connected to a tube that led to some machine into my heart, and the other needle I held over my chest. It didn't have that zombie effect on me though. I possessed great powers. I could turn into anything I wanted. For some reason the two men called for the grandmother of the family to come to the house, they wanted to turn her into a zombie too. When the grandmother got there I told her what the men were going to do. I told her that when they gave her the needle to put into her heart, to just put it under her blouse because they didn't pay much attention. She did what I said and we started making some kind of plans to get rid of the whole zombie thing. I then went walking up this country, farmland road, but I had incredible power so my walking was very fast, like 50 miles an hour. I soon approached the two men who were with the kids and I turned around and started running to the house to tell the grandmother that the two men were coming. I ran at 165 miles an hour. As I started getting near the house I slowed down and went into flight. I had turned into an eagle, and I was flying around. My wings were enormous and so powerful. I then came back down, and turned back into myself, and went into the house to warn the grandmother. When the men came in, I hid behind the door. I can't remember very well what happened after that. Except, I was trying to fly in the house to demonstrate my abilities, but the house was too small to fly around in because my wings were so huge.

First, note the very detached way in which Sarah describes her relationship to the family ("I was part of *a* family that lived there"). The two men in the dream are obviously her father and stepfather. They turned people into zombies, undoubtedly symbolizing the incest. Moreover, they were trying to destroy a little girl's "heart." But since this little girl uses denial, "it didn't have the zombie effect on me. I possessed great powers." Of course, in comparison to Karen (who was turned into a zombie), the statement is true. But it reflects generally the common phenomenon of frightened and insecure children creating fantasies of omnipotence. This dream also has a "twist of fate." Sarah's grandmother is clearly significant, but it is Sarah who is doing the saving. Unfortunately, although Sarah herself was in great need of saving, it was not yet apparent to her.

I never got involved in any weird sex while I was a prostitute. That only happened recently. About two years ago I was visiting a girlfriend in Marin county. It was a strange time for me . . . no sex, no masturbation, nothing. But I was having this one fantasy. It involved making love to this blonde woman. I actually had dreams about it. In my fantasy, I would go down on her, and caress her. It was almost an obsession. I was trying to absorb as much of her as I could. It was like I was trying to superimpose myself on her. I also noticed that this fantasy was making me have a very strong attraction to women again. Not just for the thrill thing, but for a relationship. I then realized that something was missing from my life. That I wasn't doing something right. I was avoiding all sexual confrontations because I didn't feel equipped to deal with them. But it was making me obsessed.

Anyway, this was my frame of mind when I went to visit Marin county. And wouldn't you know it . . . I met someone . . . my friend's professor. He invited us both over for tea. It was very strange because he was putting out very strong sexual messages to me, even while my girlfriend was there. I wanted to leave, but my girlfriend wanted to stay; he was talking about some book he was writing. Eventually we both left, but my girlfriend said to me, "Why don't you stay with him?" I was afraid for some reason . . . so I left with her. But once we were home, I felt compelled to go back . . . to sort of confront something in myself. I called him and said that I lost something, and that perhaps coming back to see him would help me find it . . . facilitate my coming to terms with it.

When I got back to this professor's house, we talked for a while. I told him about my discomfort, that I felt that I had lost something . . . and maybe a situation could be created to help me put everything together. He told me "Okay, close your eyes, we're going to do a little guided imagery." It was like a little seánce. The imagery has to do with walking down a road and having a hole in the sack that I was carrying. All the grain was falling out . . . and before I knew it, I had lost it all. And dogs were eating it on the road. Somehow . . . this image turned into a carcass. In the carcass was this woman. She was trying to move out of the carcass, but she was being pulled back in . . . out, and in again. To me, it was very significant . . . because she was a blonde woman. I interpreted this as my trying to deny the female part of me . . . since I wasn't having any sexual relationships. I guess it was tied up with the idea of being a female, that is, I'm not a woman unless I'm pursuing a relationship, so I had to discard that part of me. After that realization, I didn't have the blonde women dreams, or fixations with women's bodies.

After the guided imagery, the professor (his name was Brian) wanted to give me a massage. So I got undressed and he put some oil on me. It sort of burned . . . I don't know what it was. But Brian took this massage very seriously, even though he was smoking marijuana. It bothered me that he was getting stoned. I don't like the idea of intoxication before sex. After Brian stopped the massage, he went into the bathroom. When he came out, he was carrying this small sachet. The sachet had little whippy things on it. He then started massaging me again, but he was also whipping me with the sachet. If this was "whipping," I could barely feel it. I guess it was more symbolic. After he was done, he asked me how I liked being "whipped" (laughs).

I knew Brian was trying to be nice to me. But when I

looked at him, he was bruised all over his body. God knows what people were doing to *him*. He then wanted me to close my eyes and go into the bedroom. But once I got near the bedroom, I felt that something risky could happen. I guess I finally decided to go in. As I rested on the bed, he proceeded to tie one leg to one side of the bed, and one leg on the other side . . . spread-eagle. It was very "dramatic."

So there I was, laying on my back, tied to this bed. Part of me was just watching what was going on, being very interested. But there was a part of me that absolutely hated being tied down. You know . . . I actually hate small rooms and being held down. I even found myself struggling at a certain point. But then I said, "Why am I struggling? . . . Why not just relax?" So I just relaxed and it was okay. This may not sound significant . . . but to me it was . . . because I hate being tied down. I then felt a profound trust for Brian and this whole situation. I even felt that this ritual could be considered an act of love. It just depended upon my surrendering to the feeling.

Of course, Brian started whipping me again. This time at my genitals. I assume that this was supposed to have an extraordinary effect upon me. But it was just hilarious. Eventually, after this whole ordeal, I asked him to kiss me. But he wouldn't . . . claiming that Americans are too oral. I think it was just an excuse for him.

Even though I started feeling a lot of trust and emotion for Brian . . . when we started having intercourse, he was very anti-arousing. He just kept trying to "beat" me. I kind of ignored this, enough to reach orgasm. But Brian didn't come. I think part of it was that he *said* he had intercourse earlier. He was also very stoned. Of course, he was having his problems . . . maintaining an erection.

After sex, Brian became very aloof . . . saying in his British accent, "Put on your panties now, and we'll go in the other room and talk." But I said, "No, over my dead body." You should have seen his expression. (I just didn't like his sudden brashness.) He then said, "Well, you're going to put your panties on right now, or I'm going to have to give you a spanking." I laughed and said, "Fuck you!" . . . but I didn't say it in an offensive way . . . I just wanted to be strong about it.

Well . . . Brian proceeded to pick me up . . . spank me . . . hold me down . . . hit me . . . and so on. I'm not really wild about being hit . . . so I struggled, and we fought for a while. But it finally got to a point where he was holding me down and spanking me. It was then that I did something that I learned when I was young. First, I tried to dissipate the pain by imagining it being spread over my entire body. After this, I felt much better. My next step was to yell: "Brian! Did you ever think to ask me *why* I wouldn't put my panties on?" He stopped, and said he never thought to ask. When I explained to him my reason—his sudden brashness—the struggle ended. I think all of this was very erotic to him.

Later on, I asked Brian if I could massage him my way . . . you know . . . without whips. As I was massaging Brian, I started to think about my earlier feelings. I realized that it wasn't sex per se that I was suppressing, but it was my sensitivity. I think I believed that without sensitivity, I wasn't feminine. I guess I discovered that being sensitive is normal, and that it doesn't always need to include sex. These thoughts somehow led to a discussion of mothers, of all people. Brian was saying that his mother was a wonderful person, but it was at the expense of being a good mother. Brian also said that he spent most of his childhood living with his aunt . . . with whom he had had sexual relations since he was seven. I had this image of a prissy little English woman spanking Brian and having sex with him.

After I left Brian, I went back to see my girlfriend in Marin. I told her what went on with her professor . . .

and she was horrified. "How could you do it?" . . . "Why didn't you stop him from doing that?" . . . "You should have made it a good experience . . . something healthy." It certainly was bizarre. This girlfriend, by the way, thinks that my whole life has been wonderful . . . marvelous. She puts me on a pedestal . . . but I'm not too comfortable with that.

Anyway . . . Brian was my one experience with "weird" sex. Fortunately, it never happened when I was a prostitute. Actually, I was lucky to get out of prostitution when I did. The police had just instituted a major crackdown. Everyone I knew in the business was getting arrested . . . even in their homes. Although this is an illegal arrest (you have to be in the act), it was still happening.

I remember how I avoided being arrested. I got this call from a guy to meet him at a hotel. But there was something strange about his voice . . . I had a feeling that I was being set up (even though I drove there anyway). We first went out to eat, but I got up to go to the car because I felt sick. My new boyfriend, Jim, was waiting for me in the car. As we sat there, I started noticing a lot of men just hanging around. They turned out to be plainclothes policemen. We saw them handcuff these other girls, so we got out of there. That was the end of that career!

I took what was left of my earnings as a prostitute and went to New York. Most of the money I either gave away, or spent recklessly. I must have had about a hundred customers . . . my career only lasted a few months. You know . . . sometimes when I am walking down a street, I will see this vaguely familiar face . . . and I'll think it was one of my tricks.

When I came back from New York, I spent a lot of time with Jim. Although we started going out while I was a prostitute, I had actually met him several years earlier in junior high school. We met again when I picked him up

hitchhiking. My car then blew a radiator hose two blocks
later. As we waited for AAA, we got reacquainted. It was
very exciting for me because I was always attracted to
him. He is very dark, which made him stand out from the
rest of the blonde Malibu crowd. He had beautiful fea-
tures. I could spend hours gazing at him.

Jim and I did lots of strange things. One time we took
some seconals and went to the Renaissance Faire. It was
very interesting . . . but I really blew it. I knocked things
over . . . made a fool of myself . . . bothered the tourists.
With Jim, it was all sex and drugs . . . but heavier on the
sex side.

At one point in this narrative, Sarah provides insight into the
benefits of her behavior. She was an honest-to-goodness celebrity
(that "wonderful, marvelous" life). How many high school girls
have had sexual relations with their father, stepfather and stepbrother? And were prostitutes, despite having an enormous inheri-
tance (and so on)? This notoriety created a powerful image—
which was apparent to many of her friends. Also, the circumstances of this book are related to a similar dynamic. I, too, was amazed
at the adversity of Sarah's upbringing. And once again, it was Sarah's willingness to *discuss* her trauma that got my attention, and as
a consequence she received the secondary gains of tacit approval,
plus more notoriety (in a covert sense) with the publication of this
book. It is clear that Sarah learned to utilize her trauma to her benefit. It made her unique—which she ultimately interpreted as being
special. And if God was testing her, she was determined to prevail.

Unfortunately, for every step forward, Sarah takes a couple of
steps backwards. Her involvement with Brian is a good example.
Even when she anticipates danger, she feels compelled to acquiesce
to it. Furthermore, she will go through enormous mental gymnas-
tics in order not to hurt someone (i.e., reject them). She hated being
tied down—but worked hard at accepting it. She even took it a step
beyond, contemplating whether it could be an act of "love." And

despite all of the silly "whipping," the "head" games, and the bondage, Sarah brought herself to a place where she could feel "a lot of trust and emotion" for Brian. It is also obvious that her struggle and fight with him, initiated by her saying "fuck you," was motivated by her desire to please him, i.e., to give him an excuse to wrestle with her and "spank" her. When she did feel pain, she indicates that she would imagine it being spread over her whole body. Undoubtedly, this was a defense against the incest—she could desexualize the behavior by spreading it to nongenital regions.

In this narrative Sarah also describes her fantasy of an attractive blond woman. She provides several interpretations, involving the suppression of either her sexuality or sensitivity. I, on the other hand, have an alternative interpretation. Attractive blond women, especially young women, have a unique place in our society: they are the quintessence of goodness. They are adored, coveted, and utilized as symbols of fresh, vibrant, attractive, and intelligent America. While much of this is certainly the product of a powerful media, it is still the case that the youthful, attractive blond woman is represented as being only one step removed from "Mom and apple pie." Consequently, I believe that the attractive blond woman in Sarah's fantasy (as it comes out of a carcass) is the emergence of Sarah's goodness. Since it is still fantasy, it is not yet realized, but I believe that Sarah's feelings about her sensitivity (as opposed to her sexuality) are a movement in that direction. Unfortunately, although this fantasy offers a glimmer of hope, it is an image which waxes and wanes. Sarah narrowly escapes arrest for prostitution, and she immediately increases her involvement with Jim—which means more sex and drugs. He is a dark, moody-looking teeenager, with large brown eyes and long hair. Jim is significant in that he represents a transition between prostitution and Sarah's "reinvolvement" in school.

> After Jim there were other affairs, with varying durations and intensity. But my next two "relationships" were with high school teachers. One of whom was a visiting

psychology professor . . . the other my chemistry teacher.

The psychology professor was a black man. He taught at a small college in northern California. He was invited to give a seminar on "death" at my high school. I guess he was invited because he was a dying man . . . he didn't have any functional kidneys.

I was very impressed by this man (his name was Charles), so I went up to talk to him. Later . . . after finding out some information about him (he was married, but living separately), I invited him to my birthday party. But I went to his house to deliver the invitation. We talked for a long time . . . rambling on for hours and hours.

The next time I saw Charles was at a costume party. I was dressed up as a nun. Afterwards, we went back to his house . . . and I asked him for a massage. I took off all my clothes and got into bed. I think he got the message, but he told me that he couldn't have intercourse. He said that he had extremely low blood pressure, and that it inhibited him from maintaining an erection. So we played anyway . . . he was great fun in bed. We just explored each other.

Charles's body was extremely interesting. He had calcium deposits and strange scars where the doctors cut off veins in his foot and arms. It was really an interesting arrangement. I also liked the attention he paid to my body. It was a very orgasmic time. Although Charles couldn't have intercourse, he could reach orgasm . . . so it was fun for the both of us. My relationship with Charles lasted several months . . . when the seminar was terminated. He went back to northern California.

The other relationship I mentioned was with my high school chemistry teacher. I think we got involved the first day of class. I dreamt the night before that I met a man . . . and was overwhelmed with a very interesting sensation . . . like someone hit me . . . like I was being absorbed in a void and then brought back.

His name was Peter. He seemed very, very intelligent
. . . but later I was to learn that he was really crazy. I remember sitting in class, listening to the strange way that
he was teaching chemistry. Talking about eastern philoso-
phies and mystic writers. Eventually, he integrated this
into the subject of chemistry.. This really stirred my interest . . . and it helped strengthen my attraction to him. So
I invited him out to dinner.

Peter said to me, "I don't know." But I assured him
that I had taken other high school teachers out to dinner.
I also told him that my mother and family were very close
to many teachers, so it was a common thing to do. Eventually, he accepted . . . and we went to this French restaurant. After dinner, I took him back to my apartment.
All of a sudden he started talking about how enlightened
the two of us were . . . that we possessed better judgment
than the rest of the people in high school. Which was
kind of strange. But we talked on for a while and then he
suddenly decided to leave. When he left, I had one of the
most "wonderful" anxiety attacks I had ever had. The
rooms started squirming, and everything started moving
around. These things were always precipitated by either
Peter or school.

I think Peter was a father figure for me. He was in an
authority position . . . and he possessed the same warm
personality as my father. I would also get asthma when
he would come to pick me up. And one time when I was
in a restaurant with Peter, I couldn't figure out where I
was. I thought Peter was my father. I guess I was always
anxious around Peter.

Peter felt that it wasn't proper for a teacher to be sexually involved with a student. So I had to literally drag him
to bed. In fact, I once put handcuffs on him, and didn't
let him go for an entire day. But I never actually said, "I
want to have sex with you." Instead, I would write him
letters telling him that I wasn't going to push him into a

relationship . . . hoping that this would make him a little more comfortable with me . . . a little more open on the social level.

Peter and I finally got it together on a school camping trip. Since my high school only had about sixty people in it, the camping trip consisted of about twenty students. I took my mother's van. It was a very windy place, with steep hills and small shrubs. It also had some hot springs. Anyway . . . Peter and I took a long walk. We were about seven miles away from everybody. But we completely forgot about the time. It got dark very quickly, and I remember us having to hike back in total blackness. When we got back to the camp, everybody else was asleep . . . I think they were very suspicious of us. I quickly went into my van and Peter went to his tent. A little while later, I heard this knock on the van door, and it was Peter. He asked if he could come in, and of course I said yes. He told me that he wouldn't have intercourse with me . . . so we had oral sex. When we were done, he went back to his tent. He was just like a "stranger in the night."

Peter lived with a woman (Kathy) who was sixteen years older than him. Kathy didn't know what was going on between Peter and I, so she invited me over to dinner. After dinner, it got late real quickly and I was kind of drunk, so Kathy asked me to spend the night. Around midnight, I started to hear these noises. Peter and Kathy were making love in the bedroom. However, this "bedroom" was only a curtain away from me. I guess I felt that, "What I'm hearing, isn't what I'm *really* hearing." It just seemed so rude to me. And I don't think that either Kathy or Peter consciously set it up so that I would hear it. But unconsciously . . . Kathy may have wanted to show me exactly where she stood . . . and where I belonged, at the end of the triangle. Although Kathy didn't know that Peter and I were sexual, she knew that we were involved in some way.

Kathy was my mother's age, so I was young enough to be her child. Thus in some respects she may not have felt threatened, because I was the "child" and she was the "woman." For Peter, it was the Garden of Eden. Whenever he felt too much pressure from Kathy, he could make a play on me. Or vice versa . . . What an idiot . . . Eventually, Kathy and I became good friends, but I didn't like the way that she was so subservient to Peter. She made him her special child. It was rather sickening.

After all of the oral sex, Peter and I finally had intercourse. I guess he felt that since the whole school knew about our relationship, it was no longer necessary to withhold things. But it was the first and last time we had intercourse. He was horrible. I felt like I was his prop . . . just an orifice. But it wasn't even "just an orifice." There was this whole drama around this particular orifice. He was the potent dynamic male . . . and I was the young girl. I guess that I wasn't expecting this whole drama. For me, there were a lot of feelings. To him, it was a conquest. Unfortunately, I did reach orgasm . . . but there's something horrible about reaching orgasm when you feel like it's being done to you. Of course, I didn't really think about this until it was over. I guess I am one of those "leap-before-you-look" types.

I didn't tell Peter any of this. I just stopped seeing him, and he got the message. But I didn't stop my feelings at that point. It just happened that we didn't have sex after that. Of course, we didn't have sex that often anyway . . . perhaps seven times throughout the entire year.

Again, there is ample evidence of Sarah's denial, assertiveness, and need to communicate. Sarah was determined to have sex with both high school teachers, and she let nothing get in her way. She initiated the contact, and made her sexual intentions very clear.

Also, she spent a considerable amount of time talking to both of these men ("rambling on for hours and hours"), which satisfied her strong need to express herself.

Where her denial is concerned, Sarah goes to great lengths to "prove" that she doesn't have feelings like other people. Take her attraction to Charles. Are we to believe that she was really sexually attracted to his scars and calcium deposits? And what about her anxiety? Since when is a disturbing experience a "most wonderful anxiety attack"?

Part of the problem is that Sarah is talking about experiences from the past. She is removed physically, as well as emotionally, from these circumstances. Moreover, her memory is undoubtedly missing details, and her glib tone certainly minimizes the trauma. This is particularly evident when we also examine her diary from this period.

Sarah indicates that she and Peter got involved the first day of class. Her diary suggests that there were strong feelings, but not mutual ones. Furthermore, her diary gives ample evidence of how disturbed Sarah was during this period of her life.

For example, the first page of her diary starts with "My Little Tune of Self-Praise":

Oh Lord, God gave me an empty head. And I will sing my praise.
 Oh Lord, God gave me a spastic body. And I will sing my praise.
My life is so nebulous oh Lordy. And I will sing my praise.
 My nerves are giving me an ulcer, oh Lordy. And I will sing my praise.
For all these things I sing and rejoice and oh Lord have MERCY!

This "tune" is followed by a small drawing, and several words:

Is Sarah sinking in the quicksand of her thought?
Poor Sarah is sinking. What shall she do?

The remainder of this page in her diary presents a similar theme. Her one reference to Peter is as follows: "Now Sarah is sexually frustrated. And Peter is her Science Teacher (isn't that great)." The rest of the page is filled with self-punitive "poems":

> Now Sarah dear, you're losing control,
>   I think you're going insane.
> Your Karma must be fucked young girl
>   Remember your fate was all up to you . . . bitch.
> And Graduation Day is such a long time away
>   And I'm not even sure if my High School Diploma
> Will make any change in this relationship.
>
> Rejected, I have been rejected
>   After I was dissected
> They found me defective
>   Because my mind was infected.

Although Peter is not labeled in either of the poems, they probably have reference to him (i.e., "relationship" and "rejected"). On the same day, Sarah wrote the following letter to Peter in her diary:

Dear Peter,
Heartwarming is the energy and enthusiasm that radiates from the depth of your soul every schoolday morning as, with stiff lower jaw you boldly face the apathetic expressions of 80% of the student body.

For you, ha this is just another daily challenge that you face openly with that famous calcium bright, skeletal smile of yours. I admire a man with teeth, especially if they're his own. Keep up the good work Peter and remember, I'll always be there in practically every class of yours rooting you on, not to mention nutrition and lunch (and after school hours too if you gave me the chance, my little peach seed).

Never fret yourself over the gossip that sometimes goes around about your teaching abilities. If worse comes to worse you can always fall back on your face. (Do you understand the attempted joke in that line?) Anyway, you're playing your role well, and I'm sure that nobody argues about that! I'm sure there are those who envy your position, standing in front of high school classes, sparking the young minds of students (*especially* some of the female percentage, and probably some of the male!). I'll never lose faith in you as a teacher, because I know you've got what it takes. I can tell by that insane, sadistic expression you sometimes reveal when expressing some kind of joy or satisfaction. You were born for this part. I know how difficult the first year of any new role can be, and usually you just aren't mellow. But I know you'll get in the rhythm of it all. Don't quit, if not for any other reason, you might find it financially inconvenient.

Your Devoted Apostle (and student), Sarah
P.S. Please take no offense in this letter. I'm sure you know that this was basically in jest. This letter was written in a mad inspiration of sarcasm and frustration.
P.P.S. All sexual overtones in this letter you may take seriously and consider in accordance with surrounding circumstances, if you so decide (which I hope you do). Sexually, I'm in no hurry, but socially I'd like to see more of you, my little raisinette.

Even at a very disturbing point in her life, Sarah's sense of humor is readily apparent. Throughout much of this diary, her humor is the only bright spot—a small ray of hope—in a sea of despair. Again, written on the same day as her poems and letter to Peter, is the following material:

Whats wrong with Sarah? She's out of control and losing touch with her mind. Sarah was always a little strange. Even when she was young she was never innocent. Nobody liked her in her schools because she's so peculiar. She's always been so strange. You know insanity seems to run in the family. Sarah, Sarah, Sarah you just don't belong. You little *worm*.

I can't help it. I just hate her. Don't you? Gross! She's so *weird*!

In a dark corner of this room there is a voice. He degrades me. He hates me. And I know he's crazy, but for some reason I believe him.

I'm not in touch.
There's no gravity
here. Part of my mind
is way beyond the clouds.
If it goes any further it will
  explode to the solar system.
But I'm still growing.

Who is that? What
is that? She's decomposing.
Pretty soon all that will be
left will be limestone.

Finally, again on the same day, are her last references to Peter:

I feel I need
this man for some reason.

I don't think I like this position I'm in. I mean something in my gut tells me "I need him, I have to find something out." Something's pushing me, but I don't know why. Is this my intuition or is it from outside energies?
Today has been very strange. I was very nervous and emotional. Part of it was due to Peter. Sometimes I can't endure.

Given the previous material, it is paradoxical that Sarah should refer to this year in high school as "In many ways, that year with Peter was fantastic." Perhaps it is testimony to how much she learned about herself, not necessarily to her experience with Peter. Her narrative discloses much anxiety, which is further extended in her diary. A couple of months after the previous material (December 25, 1974) Sarah writes:

Silly man; now who is this?
Tom, Dick or Harpy?

Or can this be that
so-called man of intellect,
Peter.

As her diary indicates, December 1974 was a very difficult month. On December 6 she writes:

Mother, you had me, but I never had you
I needed you, you didn't need me
So I, I just got to say good-bye, good-bye

Father, you left me, but I never left you.
I wanted you, you didn't want me
So I, I just got to say

Good-bye, Good-bye

Well, Sarah, you can't be any more open than you have. I don't
know if you can give anything else under the circumstances. If a
person or just people in general can't respond back in the same
fashion or don't feel comfortable doing so, or have their reasons or
whatever the case may be, you shouldn't let it hurt you. Some
people just aren't capable. Don't feel rejected or depressed. It's
not you. And things aren't ribbons and bows.
You don't like being dependent on anything or anybody but you
need to feel dependent every once in a while. Relax. If you keep
this up this way you'll wind up cutting everyone and everything
off. I like your PaPa. You should learn from his mistakes. Get a
hold of yourself and be strong. Look up, things aren't [that bad].

On December 8 she writes:

Sometimes you need someone to lean on for a while. I've never really had anyone. Not really. So many times I've looked to my
mother but she's too busy with Karen or Al. And I'm, she feels is
the stronger of all and so she's always leaned on me. The same
with most of my friends. And those who would let me lean would
want to smother me. I can't stand that! My grandparents are
smother-like so I never tell them how I'm feeling about this, but
instead they hang all the responsibilities of Karen and Mother on
me.

Where can I go? I'm crying out inside. Screaming! Christ, I need
somebody who won't smother me but can give a little.

Forget it, honey, there's no one. You're alone. In a very total
sense. What do you do when there's no hope?

SHIT!!!!

I'm empty

I wish someone would do some little thingie for me. Maybe just take me to bed and let me snuggle up to them all night long. I've always missed snuggling. My sister said when we were little and had to sleep together that I was a boa constrictor.

Sometimes I think maybe Peter B. No/way my little limestone. That man has a hard time being open about himself and giving himself, and he was also an only child. That usually helps.

IM DYING !!!
sinking deeper

Sarah's last entry in her diary in 1974 (December 31) was another letter to Peter:

Dear Peter,
I felt like writing you a letter and I didn't think you'd object, so I did. I believe you're in Death Valley at the moment this letter is being written. I could just as well wait til school starts again to tell you all this, but I feel like telling you now, which is ridiculous in a sense since you probably won't receive it til then anyway and I probably won't mail it. Be that as it may I'm writing to you.
   Our confrontation Thursday night made me so happy I was about to cry, and so melancholy I wanted to cry. I cried when you left. I saw no reason for you to live through it too. I was happy because you talked to me openly and truthfully of your feelings and the situation. I was deeply moved by that. I can't express the emotions I felt clearly enough. Since I met you I've experienced feelings I've never had for anyone before and it felt unfamiliar and foolish to me because I didn't really know you, yet I also felt sure I did know you. This was quite a conflict in my system. I couldn't fall asleep very well for a long time because of it. The past three or four months I've felt like someone was leading me through the dark and I couldn't see where I was being lead or who it was that was doing the leading. With all the times you've left me dangling in mid-air I would have normally dropped the whole affair, but I didn't feel in control and I didn't know where I stood. My mind kept logically telling me to let go but something else wouldn't let me. I was in a state of constant confusion, over myself and over

you and some of your actions. It was awful! I feel a bit better now, though I know there's more confusion to come.

When you talked to me Thursday this questioning love I felt was unveiled. At that time I felt such a strong release of anxiety from that built-up confusion, that it almost came out in tears all over you. I can now tell myself I love you and fully believe it and what's more I can tell you too. As strange as it may sound, I was never able to really say that before, though I felt it. I do love you and I feel a deep friendship and respect for you. That's all I can possibly say and I hope you feel all right about it.

As for my melancholy state, well, that just can't be helped. I know what you're going through now and I sympathize with you. I'd love to be closer to you but I want you to be comfortable and relaxed with everything. This waiting period will probably be good for me (somehow) anyway, and my sexual frustrations I think will be easier to tolerate now. Keep care of yourself and have a Happy New Year.

With All My Love & Respect,
Sarah

This diary adds considerable insight into Sarah's psychology. Her pain and confusion come alive. She did not saunter through these experiences with nonchalance, but anguished her way through. It is a diary of a depressed, highly self-punitive, and angry young girl—with a very poor self-image. It is also potentially suicidal ("I just got to say goodbye"), and is certainly despairing.

Sarah's drawings present a similar image—angry, but self-destructive. The "arrow woman" is a clear expression of anger and frustration. The square, hard breasts with shooting arrows are further evidence of her sexual turmoil. However, it is not certain to what extent the "arrow woman" is truly Sarah. Sarah can be assertive, but she is not particularly aggressive. Perhaps, the "arrow woman" represents a persona she would like to project, but in fact, Sarah is the shriveled, faceless, fetal woman isolated at the bottom of the drawing—drinking by herself in a barren and foreboding environment.

The "heart" drawing is equally forlorn. Sarah's heart hurts, she is saddened, and she needs love. A caller from the door (perhaps her mother) offers emotionless advice, "If it hurts, cut it out." The caller ends with ridicule, "Dummy." The sad, disturbed-looking Sarah has her heart taken out by an unfeeling and sarcastic man (undoubtedly her stepfather). Sarah's nudity is again indicative of her sexual despair.

Sarah's anger and hopelessness are particularly evident in the following statement, taken from her diary (February 29, 1975):

> I'm at the County hospital to visit Karen. Al was at the house ear-lier today while I was there. Just seeing him extremely upset me. I felt like a little girl again. I was scared and hurt. This was the man that made 10 years of my childhood a complete nightmare. This was the man that was responsible for the place Karen is in. This is the man who beat, molested, humiliated, tortured and degraded two little children long ago. Two little girls who were very loving and open and trusting. Two little girls who wanted to be loved and approved of and wanted to give love back, but it was always smeared in their face whenever they tried.
> How could he do that?
> Right now he feels he holds the upper hand in the divorce. He's cheating right and left, using every trick in the book. Lying to the lawyer, lying to his family and everyone else he has to in order to attain what he wants. Why can't he be stopped? Can't the court see he rots everything he touches?

One of the most disturbing aspects of this entry is the extent to which Sarah has internalized all the damage done by Al. *Now* it is Sarah who humiliates and tortures herself. It is also Sarah who be-lieves that she is rotting, and so on. Thus it is not surprising that Sarah has difficulty establishing a love relationship, as is evident in the turmoil surrounding Peter.

Peter is a very youthful-looking high school teacher. Sarah has several pictures of him: sitting in the lotus position in the school au-ditorium; lecturing in front of class in a pleated/rumpled shirt, with beltless dungarees; gesturing to students; and so on. He is attrac-tive, with dark shoulder-length hair and sideburns. His protruding forehead, thick eyebrows, and large brown eyes give him a pene-trating look, which tends to add substance to his small thin frame.

Obviously, he is not your "average" high school teacher. He was hired right out of college, for an "alternative" school, and this was his first year at the job. In fact, he could probably pass for a "mature-looking" high school student.

Nonetheless, Sarah indicates that Peter represented a father figure. He was certainly in a position of authority, and by education and training alone, he was far beyond high school sentiments. Peter undoubtedly also evoked feelings which were similar to Sarah's feelings about her father. Both men are attractive, youthful-looking, aloof, and bright. While Sarah's father "got away" to San Francisco, Sarah was determined to keep Peter with her. There is a very driven quality about her attachment to Peter, which is exacerbated by her own independence/dependence conflict. When he is aloof, she desperately wants him. When they finally have sexual intercourse, she withdraws and ridicules him. One cannot help but think that some of her comments about Peter are projections of her own needs, especially in reference to his "conquest" mentality. "Unfortunately, I did reach orgasm" is another statement which is consistent with her own sense of conquest. Many men do not believe that they have had sex unless they have had intercourse and orgasm. Sarah was determined to have sex with Peter and this meant intercourse and orgasm. And she was not going to "cheat" herself out of this distinction. Also, Sarah concludes that she is a "leap-before-you-look" type. I would disagree. She often has a good (but misdirected) idea of what she wants—and she does all she can to get it. Look at the relationship with Peter. He precipitated all kinds of psychological problems (feelings of being out of control, anxiety attacks, asthma), rejected her often, and toyed with her at other times—until she could prevail. And once she had "won," she turned the tables. It was certainly a gesture of anger, and if Peter symbolized her father, you can get a glimpse of her unconscious feelings toward that man.

There is one additional point I would like to make about the material discussed thus far. Much has been said about Sarah the victim. The wronged little girl who had every reason to strike back.

This feeling is particularly clear in Sarah's narrative. However, in her diary another message comes across. She feels guilty about the incest ("even when she was young—she was never innocent"). A woman who has been raped will often feel guilty, believing that she could have done something more to stop it. In this case, Sarah shows the same feeling. Could she have done more? Consequently, Sarah puts herself in a double bind, victim and maybe culprit. As will be seen later, Sarah resolves this conflict.

Sarah's narrative continues:

> Breaking off from Peter was a big drain. In fact, it was then that I started seeing my psychologist. Prior to this I had been seeing a marriage and family counselor. I really didn't tell her much. I was very secretive. But my psychologist helped me develop incredible ideas about what I wanted to be involved in. That's when I decided that I wanted to go into psychology. I know I had a sense of identity, a sense of direction, but after Peter, I lost it. I guess Peter was giving me that sense of direction, he facilitated situations for me. In many ways, that year with Peter was fantastic.
>
> While I was with Peter, my sister Karen was in and out of institutions. In fact, she just recently got out of one. She is now living with her boyfriend at his family's house in Malibu. It is a very nice situation. Everything is basically stable for her. But . . . I don't feel comfortable about it. Everytime something bothers her . . . she goes off again. It's like tweedle-dee and tweedle-dum.
>
> My psychologist is a very interesting personality. He usually has a very strong impact on people. I liked him, and respected him, even though he would irritate me. I guess he was a father figure. You know, at the time I was seeing him, I didn't think that he had a very significant role in my life. But afterwards, I realized that he had a

very strong impact on me. He was influencing many changes. For instance . . . I became more spiritual, with sort of science undertones. I also got interested in numerology . . . and meditation. It was a time of shifting gears . . . formulating what I wanted to do with my life, what I wanted to be.

Somewhere along the line I got a feeling of who I was . . . apart from everything that I've done . . . or who my parents were. I also felt that it was important for me to develop even further. And actually, I started feeling more familiar with the essence of everything that I was learning. It was about this time that I had my first peak experience.

My first peak experience is a very hard thing to describe. It's like getting your first healthy orgasm . . . shaking all over (laughs). Yes, if you could characterize it, that's basically what it feels like. Of course, this description doesn't do justice to the experience. It's not like something sort of happens . . . it took a long time to build up. Probably a few months, with an acute build-up a few days beforehand. When it happened, I didn't have the vaguest idea of what was going on. But it was extremely interesting. I guess certain things happen and somehow you feel that there is truth in it.

This peak experience lasted three to four days . . . day and night. At the time, I wasn't even aware that this was a "peak experience." I had never heard of the term. But I had many strange experiences. At one point, I felt that I was a tree which was two or three thousand years old. But usually, my senses were generally heightened. There was an acute awareness of everything . . . kind of like what people describe when they take hallucinogenics. There was also an extreme clarity. But I didn't see God . . . although I felt that I was God. There was no separation. In fact, everything was God . . . the ocean . . .

Even though I was having all of these experiences, I still knew who I was. I just had this added sense of wholeness. I was one with everything. And there was a feeling of joy, even though I saw all the tragedies within my family . . . my life, and so forth. It was a perspective that I can't explain . . . it's very hard.

In some ways, it was all part of a song. The song that people feel in general . . . the stupidity that is in their minds, in other peoples' lives. Besides the song, I also experienced God as a void or absence of time, that is, not playing an important role. If God is there, it doesn't make much of a difference.

This peak experience also gave me a strong sense of purpose. I felt that it was very important that I use this period of time correctly. I wasn't going to get a chance like this again for a while. There were certain things which I had to immediately change. I also felt that I was being catapulted. One of the things that I changed was that I threw all of my drugs away, and stopped smoking. There also seemed to be a change in the structure of the way that I thought. Of course, for many of the changes, I wasn't exactly sure of why I had to make them. I guess I felt that it would become clear, even if it took a few years.

Fortunately, this peak experience only lasted a few days. It was so horrible. Actually it wasn't horrible, just bizarre. I wasn't used to it . . . like seeing people formulate thoughts. It's interesting, I didn't see whole pictures of people formulating thoughts . . . only little vortexes. I would also hear seconds before people would say something and then see it manifested through them. It really sounds crazy (laughs) . . . but it was interesting.

I know some people will think this was a psychotic episode, and not a peak experience, but where I am now speaks for itself. I've made many changes . . . envisioned from that experience. That experience had purpose . . .

and gave me balance and stability. Also, the experience didn't frighten me, although the visual part was a bit frightening. In fact, the experience was less frightening in part because my psychologist told me that it was a good thing.

When I learned about "peak experiences," I discovered that people in the past had similar episodes. However, in many of these other cases, God had much to do with it. Like touching people on the head. I guess it was glorified as something very special . . . God made you an oracle. But I don't see it that way. I see it as a direct evolutionary process. In the past, there were fewer such experiences. But now, they are more and more common. That is, we are getting closer to being that God . . . recreated from a thousand years ago. In many ways, it is just a normal process of getting closer to being gods.

All of these ideas had a strange effect on everyone I knew. My teachers were being blown away by this . . . saying that I couldn't cope in school . . . everything was falling apart into a big mess. But . . . I turned it all around. I became a big achiever . . . very active in school and doing many things. Of course, some teachers knew all the time that I could cope, but I don't think that they expected such a big change . . . and so abruptly. And it lasted, it was a whole change. It gave me grounding. Before that I was so scared . . . I had lots of ideas, but no organization . . . everything was stirring. But I made it that year . . . and then I went to Switzerland for the summer (laughs).

Why did Sarah change? What was it about the relationship with Peter that precipitated this turn of events? I have several ideas. First, Sarah hardly benefited from her pursuit of Peter. She suffered, and in the end, it was never satisfying. Consequently, she may have examined the relative merits of pursuing such men, given the emotional costs. Secondly, if Sarah was trying to prove a point, such as "recapturing" father, she may have once again evaluated what it required to achieve this questionable goal. In each of these cases Sarah may ultimately have recognized the futility of her actions. She had unresolved conflicts with her father, stepfather and mother—and Peter was a poor substitute for resolution. He only caused her pain. Furthermore, what little advantages she may have gained from rejecting or ridiculing Peter were more than offset by her emotional turmoil. In short, Sarah got some insight.

This is clearly a period of emergence for Sarah, an existential transition point. She is striving toward a future state of self-fulfillment, benefiting from her own phenomenology. Her "peak experience" is one example. The term "peak experience" comes from the work of Abraham Maslow (1908—1970). It generally refers to an experience which is characterized by: feelings of wholeness; perceptual sensitivity; feelings of self-validation, self-justification, and goodness; disorientation in time and space; feelings of wonder, awe, reverence, humility, and surrender; and finally, feelings of godliness.[1] From Sarah's description, it appears that she is justified in using this terminology. Moreover, she received additional validation from her psychologist about the significance of this event.

Perhaps the most significant outcome of Sarah's peak experience is her feeling of independence. She realized that she is not a slave to her past. Her childhood was tragic, but the emerging Sarah can create a better future. This feeling acknowledges both the sympathy she deserves, plus the encouragement she needs. She suffered, and then rebelled. Sarah could continue this way (and everyone would understand and pity her)—or she could stop trying to "even the score." Sarah is now moving toward the latter. She is feeling better about herself, is accepting the help of an appropriate and nonsexualized father figure (her psychologist), and is trying to understand her own place in a broader perspective than her immediate family (God, cosmology, etc.).

Sarah surprised many people. Her turnaround was drastic—

1. P. R. Abramson, *Personality* (New York: Holt, Rinehart & Winston, 1980).

and unexpected. She used a strange and disorienting experience to further her achievement. She did not drop out, withdraw into a cult, become a religious fanatic, and so on. Instead, she decided to devote herself to studying and becoming more active in school functions.

Sarah's narrative continues:

> I guess at this point I decided that I wanted a more formal high school education. I wanted a rigorous academic setting, and I was afraid that I would never have it at my "alternative" school. It was the end of my senior year, and Karen had been to this wonderful school in Switzerland (it was in an enormous estate, overlooking a lake), so I decided to attend. Actually, this school often sent Karen home because she was so unstable. She was really an outcast. She had pierced her nose and dressed really strangely . . . and in a conservative country like Switzerland, it was really outrageous.
>
> This school in Switzerland has an international reputation, and is for girls only. The girls were often from European nobility, or wealthy Arab families. There were only a few Americans. My family learned about the school through my psychologist, who was a friend of the owners. I think the school was also an international center for psychoanalysis.
>
> This school was a little hard to get used to since it was highly regimented. Besides the structure, you needed a counselor's permission to spend the evening out. Usually you had to be in by 9:00 PM But . . . this school was the first time that I felt *real* peace. I mean there was no tension. It was really incredible for me. Actually, the only bad experiences I had were associated with Karen. They didn't really throw her out, she died (laughs). That is, she was almost in a coma. She didn't eat or drink . . . and she

looked crazy, with the ring through her nose, bracelets up to her elbows . . . massive make-up . . . bright red clown lips. And she would always stare straight at people . . . never trying to make herself liked.

The other thing that I liked about the school was that I had my own private space. I mentioned earlier how strangers were always showing up at my mother's house. Well . . . they also seemed to find me when I lived in Venice (California). I remember this one time, this young man showed up at my apartment . . . he was a neighbor's friend. He asked me if he could stay for a while, and I said okay. I didn't know at the time that he was wanted by the FBI. It seems that he was an accomplice in a robbery (to steal antique pipes) in California, and I guess he transported the stuff, plus himself, to Florida. When he came back to California, he was very shy and didn't talk very much. He was also going through a divorce . . . his wife was turning tricks in Hollywood.

This guy was very nervous. He had been talking with his parents' minister, trying to buy time until he tied up all of his affairs. He was then going to turn himself in. But his parents called the police and told them where he was staying (at my apartment). When the police arrived, I was at school. I later learned that my apartment was under surveillance. I was never implicated for helping a fugitive because the minister told the police that this guy was just settling some things so that he could turn himself in.

I never had sex with this fugitive. I sure tried, but he saw me as being instrumental in turning himself in, and didn't want to get involved. I used to write him letters when he was in jail . . . I even went to visit him once. It was a strange encounter. I was waiting and waiting, but he wasn't showing up at the visitors' station. Then I noticed someone in back who looked like him but was talking to this woman. The woman turned out to be his wife. She promised to stop tricking, and they were talking about getting back together. She looked lower-middle class to me . . . and she looked like she got married too young. But she didn't look like a prostitute.

It's funny, most men I knew didn't have the faintest idea of what a prostitute really looks like. The only person I ever knew who looked like the stereotype of a prostitute was my friend Patti. In fact, my male friends used to tell me to stay away from Patti . . . "Don't hang around with her type" . . . "What are you doing in this kind of business? Don't worry, I'll put you through school." As I mentioned before, Patti didn't fare too well. Besides the heroin, she also got beat up. Eventually, she married this gay artist from England. Boy, did they have an incredibly bizarre wedding! Her husband and his male lover got into these pantyhose and did a water ballet act in the pool. Patti was high on angel dust . . . and the minister was making passes at all the half-naked women. All the gay guys were making passes at the minister. And for entertainment (if this wasn't enough), the San Francisco Cockettes were there. They are a theater group of transvestites who were the most well-behaved people at the party.

This marriage didn't last. Patti is now living with some other guy, and she has three children . . . all of whom were born while she was taking drugs.

These were the kinds of scenes I left behind when I went to Switzerland. When I knew that I was leaving the country, I did have one last fling. My grandparents had given me money to buy some clothes, so I went to this store in Beverly Hills that was having a sale. It was not a well-situated store, and very few people came in. Only one man worked there. I can't remember what led up to the incident, but I wound up feeling sorry for this guy because no one came into the store. Oh . . . I remember what happened. I was trying on some pants in the dressing room and he came in. We didn't say very much, except things like, "Would you like to have sex?" "Would you like to have it in here or there?" I chose the spot. It was on his boss's desk. I felt that the desk was a less obvious place than the dressing room, which was visible from the store window. It was bizarre, and I didn't enjoy this guy's nervousness. I guess his boss was expected back soon. This place, by the way, shortly went out of business.

Well anyway . . . Switzerland. It is such an incredible place . . . spotless! Clean, with everything being very orderly . . . and on time. To me, it was heaven, because my life was a scattered mess. I loved it.

My school in Switzerland had a number of very bright girls. Actually, I don't know if this indicates brightness, but many of the girls were bilingual, with some knowing up to four languages. But there were dumb people there too. The dumbest were the girls from New York. There was also one from West Lake (California) who was such an asshole . . . she was very dumb. She was also very sheltered, and lasted for only two weeks. I guess she just couldn't handle being away from her family.

I was only in Switzerland for about seven weeks. I took the summer school session. I had the option to stay, but I decided to come home. I mostly took language classes (I'm fluent in French), which lasted four hours a day. Other than class, I took it easy, or did recreational things.

I had one sexual experience while I was in Switzerland. I had just seen *One Flew Over the Cuckoo's Nest*, dubbed in French, and walked to a little carnival. This South American man was telling these girls about a time when he was living with a primitive tribe. He asked if there was anyone who wanted to see films of this. I was interested in seeing his films, but no one else came along. When we got to his place, I noticed that there wasn't any film projector. There were however, pornographic pictures on the wall. I remember stressing to this man that I was trusting him . . . and that he would dishonor himself if he was taking me for a "ride." But he said, "Ah, no, no, no." So I said all right, but asked him about the projector. He told me that his friend was bringing it, so I decided to wait. I told him that I was inclined not to believe him, yet for honor's sake, I would stay for half an hour. During this half-hour he kept making polite advances toward me. And about two minutes before I was to leave I started yielding to his advances. When his pants were down to his knees, and he had an erection . . . I left. That was my big sexual experience in Switzerland.

One of the things I learned at this school was that sex could not be taken casually. Here, it was absolutely wrong. I guess I started learning a certain amount of responsibility for my sexual relations. You just don't have sex for many reasons.

I left Switzerland feeling very good. In fact, I had my second "peak experience" when I arrived back in Los Angeles. I guess I was moving in the "peak" direction during my time in Switzerland. Like . . . although I used to have many physical problems (I'm hypoglycemic), I never felt healthier or more energetic. My usual uncomfortableness and inertia were gone. When I arrived back in LA (actually Karen was with me), it was two in the morning and no one knew that we were coming in. But it was strange. Although it was 2 AM Tuesday, and nothing was going on, I could really feel the intensity of the city. I also wondered how anyone survived here . . . It was amazing to me. But it's so hard to explain, because this doesn't sound like something that would galvanize into a great insight. But I guess that I was thinking in terms of the whole world, where somebody is a small concentrated thing. I also had the same timelessness, and ancientness as before. But with *this* peak experience, there were no fireworks . . . it was just an acute awareness . . . a very strong feeling of purpose, rather than the more abstract feeling that I had before. This peak experience also took on a very planetary meaning to me . . . everybody in Los Angeles had no relation to my body, but had a relation to my mind. My mind was merely an instrument for me . . . all of which I translated into a certain "purpose."

I talked about this second peak experience with my new psychologist. Her name was Diane. Diane brought me through a special visualization. As I closed my eyes, I immediately saw an image of the crucifixion. I guess it was my Catholic upbringing. But what was strange about the crucifixion was that *I* wasn't being crucified. I wasn't the body . . . I was the light. And the word that came to me was "Transfiguration" . . . which means a whole array of different things in different contexts. But to me, transfiguration meant that I was myself . . . but that I wasn't myself. That is, I wasn't myself as I am.

I've often wished that I had more knowledge during that peak experience. I could have given such good forms to the things that were coming to me. But I guess that it was a marking place for me . . . a taste of something to work toward. I was enveloped in this feeling for about a month, and then it subsided. It wasn't like the feeling actually left me, but the intensity subsided. And once the intensity was gone, everything felt blah . . . and empty. I was hollow again. Of course, that is just an illusion created by the difference between the intensity and my normal state.

I also felt a special closeness during this period. When I saw my mother, she wasn't my mother. I mean she was physically my mother . . . and physically my friend. But there was no separation. It was the kind of closeness you feel with a very special member of your family . . . connectedness. This connectedness extended everywhere. It was incredible.

Switzerland was a very special place for Sarah. It appealed to her need for structure, compulsiveness, and charm. Her school brochure also suggests that it was a place of refined elegance. The building is a large, eighteenth-century baroque estate overlooking Lake Lugano. The amenities included an Olympic-size swimming pool, water skiing, sailing, horseback riding, arts and crafts, skiing, dances, athletics, music, and cooking. One or two photographs also implied that academics were involved. Undoubtedly, this was both a nice respite and pleasant reward for Sarah's renewed interest in achievement.

Karen was not so fortunate. The splendor and structure of Switzerland were little consolation for her inner turmoil. In a photograph from that period, Karen looks unquestionably strange. Her face, half-heartedly accentuated by both of her hands, expresses a "take-a-look-at-this" attitude. And what she is showing is: a diamond stud pierced through her left nostril; large half-moon earrings; bright red lipstick; dark eye shadow—topped with a bouffant hairdo. She is also wearing a hot pink dress, a white ermine coat, and ten bracelets on her left arm. It is no wonder that she had a difficult time in Switzerland. In contrast, Sarah was feeling good about herself, worked productively—and impressed people. This last comment is in reference to a recent letter Sarah received from the owners of the school asking her if she would consider teaching there. Obviously, Sarah was not held responsible for Karen—even though I'm sure that Sarah felt guilty about her inability to mollify Karen (i.e., "They didn't really throw her out, she died [laughs]").

Despite her first peak experience, Sarah managed to find trouble. Nurturing the downtrodden was translated into "sex with the unfortunate." Sarah toyed with the South American man, reminding him of his honor; she persisted in trying to sleep with the fugitive; and she felt sorry for the employee in the clothing store. Altruism can go only so far, and Sarah eventually limited this kind of behavior. In Switzerland, she accepted the tenet that "sex should not be taken casually," and most of her subsequent relationships involved emotional commitments.

Sarah also indicates she had a second peak experience on her return to Los Angeles. Two themes developed: the importance of her mind, and the need to establish closeness. Sarah mentions she felt that "everyone in LA had no relation to her body, but had a relation to her mind." I believe that this symbolized her recognition of the futility of indiscriminate sex. She is now going to relate mentally, before other types of involvement. This theme is also evident in the "crucifixion/transfiguration" imagery. She is no longer the "body," but instead, is the light.

Sarah's need for closeness is also related to the "importance of her mind." She has been using sex to create intimacy, as well as to express anger and rebellion. Now, she wants to change this. She wants to feel close to people in situations other than sex. The second peak experience signifies to her that she can become connected with people without recourse to sexual intercourse.

Unfortunately, Sarah's intentions are more admirable than her actions. This is real life, where insight and change are a slow process filled with setbacks and doubts. Sarah makes progress, but it is by no means immediate. The narrative continues:

> After this peak experience I entered college at UCLA. But I had so many different thoughts on my mind . . . my mother . . . old boyfriends . . . Switzerland. In Switzerland, although they are strict and conservative on the surface, they all have ghosts in their closets. I remember talking to my mother about this . . . and about sexual things that I used to do (like giving someone head in the middle of the road). It's funny, I can talk to my mother about these things . . . and she takes it so casually. I guess it

has given me a playful attitude about sex. I remember in junior high school . . . I used to sneak up behind boys and pull their pants down. I once got knocked across four desks for doing that. I didn't feel it, because I was laughing so hard.

In the beginning, UCLA was a letdown for me. I was used to having fantastic teachers. People who believed that teaching was an art. I remember this woman high school teacher I had was absolutely inspiring . . . she really made you think. She also had a way of asking questions and presenting things that was incredible. I used to sit in awe watching her. I guess I made heroes out of many of my high school teachers.

At UCLA I had my first really horrible teacher. He was a math professor . . . who was just the worst. He couldn't speak English and half the things he put on the board he would erase, saying that they were wrong. But I did have a very good humanities class. The teacher was wonderful . . . she was very enthusiastic. I guess it was also hard for me to get used to the idea of taking one or two tests within a very short period . . . and having your knowledge based on only those two performances. I did okay though, and had a B average for my first quarter.

The nicest thing at UCLA was the vast and diverse population of students. It was just wonderful. I really liked meeting and sleeping with all different types of people. There was this one guy who was a psychology major. He looked like a cornhusker . . . and was a bodybuilder. I remember hearing some girls talking about him as an example of an older boy who was still a virgin. Of course, he wasn't. Anyway . . . it's funny how people create sexual stereotypes.

Another guy I went out with told me he was engaged. I don't know why men tell me things like that. I really wish they wouldn't. Anyway, his fiancée showed up one night when he was just about to penetrate me. I guess sometimes I'm too far removed from these situations . . . because I found it so funny that I landed on the floor laughing.

Although there were many other men, one of my more intense relationships was with another woman. Her name was Beth and she was several years older than me. I met her through a friend of my mother's. Several of my friends told me she was gay but I didn't think much of it. I also didn't catch on when she started making overtures toward me. Actually, I later found out that she had had an affair with my mother's friend *and* her daughter. My mother's friend was in her fifties. Beth usually liked older women. I think part of it was that the older women stood for mother figures.

I have no idea what Beth gets out of sex with older women. To me, I have such an adverse reaction to it. When opportunities come my way, I feel like, "Oh my God, it's like having sex with my mother." I guess there couldn't be a more dominant figure in my life. But then I do have sex with older men. I guess that could be like having sex with your father . . . but he wasn't around much so it doesn't bother me. Of course, sex with an older man is more culturally accepted.

I can't really remember how Beth and I got started. I thought she was coming on to me, but I couldn't tell. Sometimes I'm really dense. She never came up and grabbed my crotch, or said something like, "I'll go down on you, if you go down on me." That's a male stereotype . . . the macho kind of thing.

I think what probably happened is that she was giving me a massage with a little more enthusiasm than I had anticipated. I was naked . . . but everybody in the house was naked all of the time. My mother's friend (Julie) actually let Beth live with her because Beth was the lover of

her oldest daughter (Mary). Although Julie had a boyfriend, she also had a short affair with Beth. This sounds
like a soap opera (laughs). Anyway, Mary also found a
boyfriend and eventually left the house . . . but Beth
stayed on. So when I used to visit Julie, I also spent a lot
of time talking with Beth. Beth and I had a lot in common
. . . humanistic psychology . . . biofeedback . . . spiritual-
ism. Actually, Beth is now doing a master's at a small
Catholic college in Los Angeles (laughs).

I really liked Beth. She has a face like the little animal
in *Alice in Wonderland* that goes in the tea pot. She has
dark reddish-brown hair and brown eyes . . . Italian descent. She is also quiet and very shy. Not at all a gay stereotype . . . and certainly not like a "butch dyke."

That reminds me . . . I once had this confrontation
with a "butch dyke" motorcyclist in Venice. I was in this
weird bar that we used to call the "Dead Rat Cafe." Anyway, this dyke said to me (mimicking a deep masculine
voice), "Hey, Babe . . . I really like you . . . Hey, watcha
doing?" Stuff like that. And she was gigantic! I don't
think there was a piece of loose flesh on her . . . She was
a mass of muscles. Of course, it would have been okay if
she just left me alone. But she was being so aggressive
. . . and I was trying to be polite. I guess somewhere
along the way she got insulted because I stuck out my
boob (laughter). We got out of there after that.

Oh yeah . . . as I mentioned before, Beth was giving
me a massage. Although she didn't do anything sexual, it
became apparent to me that sex was involved. This didn't
really arouse me . . . but it surprised me . . . in both a
pleasant . . . and an adverse way. We had a close relationship and we used to talk a lot . . . but this experience
made me confront things within myself. You know, I believe that people are intimidated by homosexuals because
they force them to look at something within themselves
which they have to make a decision about. I guess Beth

made me a little uncomfortable. She was stroking me and caressing me, and I had to assume that sex was on her mind. But I didn't say anything to her. You know, it is ironic to me . . . none of the other women I was sexual with . . . they never had anything in common with Beth. Of course, I didn't have sex with that many women . . . although I certainly tried (laughs). I guess I was unpopular at one point toward the end of high school because I used to come on to all of the girls. Especially the ones who batted their eyelashes and wiggled their stuff. They were so cute. They would also flirt with me, but at a certain point . . . like when I would kiss them or pull up their shirts . . . they would say, "What are you doing?"

You know most of the women before Beth . . . I would come on to them at parties. It always seemed easier at a party. However, I tended to be more aggressive with men . . . I think I was a little scared of women . . . so a party made it easier. Also, most of my ménages à trois, and my one orgy occurred at a party. It's funny, the orgy happened when I was sixteen years old. People were getting stoned . . . and bored . . . so they started having sex. There was this one person who kept giving me the eye, but I didn't get a good feeling from him. Once we got in the bedroom, he darted right for me. But he had this huge penis . . . which I couldn't accomodate. I was in pain and I was screaming ("Help, stop"), but nobody knew what was going on. It was really close to rape . . . but I guess the situation condoned this kind of behavior.

I'm not sure why I was ambivalent about Beth's sexual intentions. In fact, my ambivalence was quite shocking to me. I loved her a great deal . . . and in the past everything was wonderful. But I still can't figure it out . . . it wasn't like I was afraid of losing control . . . and I felt that her initiation of things was delightful. However, it was after Beth that I decided that I wasn't gay . . . and that it wasn't fair for me to have a relationship with a woman

. . . given that I couldn't have a relationship with a woman like I could have with a man.

After Beth gave me the massage, I started talking to her about my frustrations with past relationships. Some time after that we started having sex. But I couldn't feel a thing. It was like my body was absolutely numb. It was shocking . . . my body had never gotten numb before. I actually talked with my male psychologist about this . . . I was very upset . . . not knowing what was wrong. My psychologist was not in favor of homosexuality. He's not against it on an individual level . . . but he didn't condone it for me.

It was so strange with Beth. I couldn't feel her when she touched me. I couldn't feel her when she went down on me. I mean I could feel her . . . but my body was turned off. It was like someone had turned off a light. Of course, she enjoyed it. It was a wonderful experience for her. But for me, nothing . . . and the bizarre thing is that it kept happening. I didn't have performance anxiety . . . but I did have anxiety. Yet I felt that there was no reason why I should be uncomfortable. I couldn't figure it out. Even though other people are uncomfortable about homosexuality, I was never raised according to the "iron fist" credo that homosexuality is horrible.

You know . . . it has taken me a long time to trust the way I feel. Even now, I still have to wait awhile. But with Beth . . I didn't know what was going on. The only time I wasn't tense is when we had a ménage à trois with a psychiatrist friend of hers. His name was Tom and he lived in Topanga Canyon. He had called Beth and asked her, "Why don't you and your girlfiriend come over for a while?" I guess he also mentioned something about a ménage à trois. I didn't know about this, but I knew that Beth was close to him, so I said, "Well, okay, what the hell!" this was still a time when I wasn't thinking . . . I felt that I could walk into any situation . . . regardless of how incredible it was.

When we got to Tom's, he was still working. So we went into the hot tub. Tom's wife also had her boyfriend over, but they were in another part of the house. I guess this marriage was working . . . Tom and his wife stuck together and they seem to still love and respect each other. But I don't know how wonderful it is for their three-year-old son. He was in yet another bedroom. . . asleep.

After we got out of the hot tub, Beth went in to see Tom. I left for a short while to do an errand. When I returned, Tom and Beth were smoking marijuana. As soon as I came into the room, all actions turned toward me. Beth put her arm around me and started coming on. I was comfortable with this . . . but when Tom got involved, I started to get nervous. I was in a very strange mood. I think I left the room. It seemed to me that Tom was only doing things for Beth . . . so I wasn't missed.

Afterwards, Beth, Tom, and I talked in the kitchen. I felt that we were all connected, sharing the same experience. There were no lights on, and I can still remember the shadows . . . Tom's spider legs . . . Beth's back. I also remember that Beth told Tom that I was into psychological things. He said "Oh, shit!"

As I mentioned earlier, after Beth, I realized that I wasn't gay . . . and that I shouldn't have affairs with women. Once I had this revelation I felt more comfortable with her, even though I didn't have sex with Beth anymore. I guess if I did have sex with her, the fear that I was gay might creep back in. You know . . . I never had this fear before. When I was sixteen, there wasn't a strong distinction between my sexual feelings for men and my sexual feelings for women. Much to my surprise, it came later. And when I finally decided not have sex with Beth anymore . . . she wasn't very happy. She loved me . . . and I was her primary relationship. It wasn't until I started backing out that she got involved with Tom.

Beth is the type of person who throws everything into a relationship. When I ended ours, she stopped working and going to school . . . and actually went to New York for a while. As I mentioned before, she is back and trying to get a master's degree. But I felt very sad when it was over . . . even though I probably felt sad for me. I really didn't want to leave her . . . I just felt so uncomfortable. After Beth, I decided to make a point of not having a relationship for a while.

Given the previous passage, we may question the validity of Sarah's "peak experiences," wondering, what kind of changes has she made? The indiscriminate sex has not vanished, she involves herself in dubious relationships, and she is far from the "path of enlightenment." However, as I indicated earlier, this is real life, where progress is slow, and setbacks and doubts persist.

Sarah's second peak experience occurred in August 1976. She entered UCLA the following month and started her affair with Beth in January 1977. The affair was over within three weeks. Thus, in this previous section, Sarah is talking about a period of only six months.

Despite Sarah's fallibility, I believe that she is still making progress. Obviously, given her upbringing, it is going to be slow. But she is moving in the right direction. As an example, look at her affair with Beth. Sarah ended this relationship *shortly* after feeling very uncomfortable. Something was wrong, and it did not take her a year to admit it. On Febuary 9, 1977 (from her diary) she is despairing:

I feel like I'm dying. I remember a few weeks ago, I was contemplating my 1977 image and before me my winged lion with forehead ablaze was running and breaking through this succession of round wires with paper stretched out over them. He was plowing through a seemingly endless row of them. Actually they stopped once they twined their way around this corner.

I think I now know what that image was all about. I feel like an onion whose skins are being pulled away one by one.

I feel almost like I'm looking death straight in the face, but I don't die, I just keep on existing in agony. A car almost hit me, practically head on, and only barely missed. I found myself regretting that he hadn't killed me, or just put me in a long peaceful coma.

After class today I went home and ate lunch and sat back to rest for awhile. I was feeling just a bit on the emotionally stimulated side. I started feeling that gruesome overwhelming feeling, once again. I tried relaxing and meditating, but I could feel myself so sensitive to overstimulation I refrained from even attempting any energy transmutations or direct conscious contact with the radiating center above my head. I just meditated on serenity and pictured myself in blue light, then said aloud, "I stand a point of peace" . . . etc. It helped, but not for that long.

I started going into hysterics again at about 5:00 PM It consisted of wanting to tear my skin off (I did tear my clothes off), taking off all my jewelry, and beating the bed concurrently with hysterical screaming and crying. I felt so exhausted with life and I wanted to rest from it, and not seeing it as possible without running away from all my responsibilities made me feel even more desperate. I didn't feel like seeing anyone or doing anything, but I invited a friend over to study for our anthropology midterm. At one point, I decided that I would put my mind into something that didn't require much concentration or any obligation. So I turned on some Bach and started making dinner. My friend came over about 6:00 PM and by 9:30 PM I was a lot better.

Now I feel almost scared to be by myself. I must not be doing something right. I can see that my life must go through some great changes or I simply won't survive the impact of the resultant friction.

Shortly thereafter, Sarah made a change. She terminated sex with Beth, and admitted to herself that homosexual behavior made her very uncomfortable. In contrast to the turmoil of Febuary 9 is her diary entry for February 13, 1977:

The major part of my hysteria is over with now, but I'm still in a rather strange frame of mind. I have to make a major change in my thought patterns. Old ways of thinking and relating to people (and situations) have to change now. When I'm with someone and I start getting into all those little things to attract a man, or a friend, or whatever else, I start feeling very strange and empty, just very strange. It isn't till I consciously put myself in group perspective that I feel released from the muck. I feel quite dirty and I guess sinful (strange word) until I do that.

Last night I had sex with a boy I really didn't think I should have. The next morning, I felt gruesome. I know I should not be sleeping with anyone, with the exception of my "cornhusker" for some reason.

I don't know, I feel so confused.

Sarah's feelings are unsettled, but her despair is now replaced with uncertainty. The heterosexual affair was probably a symbolic mark of transition. Apparently, Sarah understood that this was an inappropriate gesture.

Since the time I received Sarah's "21st Birthday" letter, I have wondered why she selected me as the recipient of this material. Her diary provides a small clue. I am mentioned only once, and it was two days after the above letter (February 15, 1977). Sarah had taken an introductory psychology course from me in the fall of 1976, where she was one of five hundred students. Not surprisingly, I barely knew who she was.

Her diary of February 15, 1977 reads as follows:

Another dream I had concerned Paul Abramson. I dreamed I was in his office and I was making him a frame for a picture I was going to give him. He helped me cut some wood in two. Then he started taking apart a collage I had done. It was of an eastern nature. I asked him why he was doing it and it was because he thought that's what he was supposed to do. I then asked him if there were any pictures in there that he would want to keep separately in his office. I showed him these two pictures of white suns or spheres. I thought they were beautiful and would induce great things to people who came to see him.

Then I think we went out to where my exam was. He was very friendly and relaxed around me, which was a change and made me feel very good. We did a lot of joking around and a lot of warm and friendly touching.

I then was asked to drive him home. I was happy to do this because it meant that he trusted me and that I could meet his girlfriend which I had wanted to do for a while. There was a lot of touching and kissing between us, which was mostly his doing. It made me feel good that I was a trusted friend now. We stopped for a while at this purely white cemetery and I straightened a crooked cross on a grave. We then went to this country sauna. It was a lousy sauna. It was too cold, although everybody else was burning up.

I was very surprised to see my name in Sarah's diary. I knew that she was a student of mine, but in a class of five hundred it is difficult to imagine having any impact on anyone. Nonetheless, I found this dream very interesting, almost prescient. Instead of taking her collage apart, I am now taking her life apart. I am also the recipient of her pictures (family, friends, etc.), and this book on Sarah is having a major impact on "people who come to see me."

This dream is also unquestionably sexual. In contrast to her previous relationships with male authority figures, it did not precipitate an invitation to dinner or massage. In some ways, Sarah has changed. However, there are other similarities between myself and her chemistry teacher Peter. It was his first teaching assignment, and mine as well. We both dressed in a casual manner, had an informal teaching style, yet remained relatively aloof. There are also some physical similarities (brown hair, brown eyes, etc.). Thus, Sarah's attraction to Peter may have been analogous to the dynamics of Sarah's attraction to me. We were both "father figures."

Additionally, I believe that Sarah was attracted to the "psychologist" in me. She had had very good experiences with her psychologists—and perhaps, she assumed that I could also facilitate her growth and change. Consequently, I believe that she chose me as the recipient of her life history because she was attracted to me as a man, and believed in me as a psychologist.

Why did Sarah dream about me shortly after she ended her affair with Beth? Obviously, Sarah needed help, and felt compelled to reestablish contact with men. Perhaps I satisfied both of those objectives. Also, terminating her relationship with Beth was symbolic of giving up "reckless abandon." Sarah could no longer rebel without censure, and it was difficult for her to face a future of integrity and responsibility. Consequently, again, the "psychologist/father/sex object" image may have been a source of reassurance.

Sarah ended the previous narrative as follows; "After Beth, I decided to make a point of not having a relationship for a while." As her diary indicates, nothing could be further from the truth. Sarah has had a growing need to stabilize her life, and combined with the trauma associated with Beth, she was "ripe" for a long-term, committed heterosexual relationship. On February 20, 1977 she met Roger. On February 28, 1977 she writes:

> I have to keep my head in the right place. I'm very susceptible towards glamour in my relationship with Roger. Even as I'm writing this the sappy sentiment is pouring in and sticking up my senses. I think part of it is due to the fact that I've had only an average of 5 hours sleep a night.
>
> It's a very hard thing for me to fathom. I'm in love. Not in infatuation, not in lust, but I have truly met "my man." I know this to be true. Maybe I'm totally deluded, but I think not. Where I am the victim of illusion concerns the relationship at the present. I should not let my mind get absorbed in visions of its development. I have to keep my head in the present. I have to preserve my head for classes. This whole thing has affected my concentration.

Sarah describes a similar feeling in her narrative:

> When I started a relationship again . . . it was with Roger. This was in my second quarter at UCLA, Roger made me feel renewed. I loved him very much and I was inspired to be monogamous. It hadn't happened in a long time. I think it was also a period of change for me . . . my previous life style was not too constructive. And there was nobody around who could top the way I felt about Roger.
>
> I remember when I went to visit my grandparents . . .

they immediately knew that I was in love. I sort of glowed. I even set up a rendezvous between Beth and Roger. Beth was curious about this person who meant so much to me.

There were only two people I loved before Roger . . . John and Glen. I guess I never told you about Glen . . . he wasn't very sexually exciting. And he didn't last that long . . . much to my shock. Actually, he was my teacher's son . . . and it was on the night of my eighteenth birthday that I committed my one and only act of statutory rape. He was seventeen. It was ridiculous.

Glen's father (my teacher) brought Glen to my birthday party. I was Glen's father's favorite student. When Glen and I started talking, he told me that he wanted to have sex. So I got my car, and I took him away from the party . . . to my apartment in Venice. I brought him back in the morning.

I was quite fond of Glen. He was very active politically. I think he was President of the Youth Chest Order of California . . . and Youth Governor of California. He was very ambitious . . . although for what purpose, I'm not exactly sure. I knew underneath . . . he was really strange. We started having problems. He was shocked by the amount of affection I had for him . . . I guess he wasn't very comfortable with it. And when we had sex, he couldn't figure out whether he did, or did not, want to be there.

Glen and I had even more problems when he was elected Youth Governor of California. We were still together . . . but he started thinking that I wasn't "presentable" enough. That I was still too "open". I remember one time he was supposed to fly to Sacramento to meet with some major politicians. There was going to be a big send-off . . . but he didn't want me there. I was very hurt. First of all, I could't believe my ears. I couldn't believe that anybody even thought that way. I guess I could actually understand someone feeling that way . . . but acquiescing to something like that is so *fucked*.

I just recently talked with Glen's family. He want to Yale . . . dropped out for a year, and then went back. His older brother tells me that it was such a mess. Glen was dropping acid (LSD). You know, when I was with Glen, I used to think that it would be great for him to take LSD. He would have me to guide him through it. But now . . . he was using LSD to avoid things . . . he has become very pessimistic. To him, everything is empty . . . our culture . . . our values . . . everything. It is all just empty gestures. I guess this is the "enlightenment" that Glen got from LSD. Fortunately, now that he is back in school, he is not taking LSD. But he is still escaping . . . this time by studying all of the time.

After Glen rejected me, I was hurt . . . but then I got furious and decided to do something in return. At first, I thought I would make sandwich boards (laughs). You know, one of the reasons that Glen told me that he didn't want me at the airport was that a lot of his political power was homosexual. And somehow, if the government people saw me there, they would not be interested in him. So . . . I was going to write that I was Glen's concubine . . . on the sandwich boards. And parade around the airport. Of course . . . I didn't go to the airport.

It was hard breaking up with Glen. Everyday that I went to school, I would see his father. It was a big junkpile. Sometime later, I saw Glen again, but all we did was quarrel. When I would be cheerful . . . this would bother him even more. But I didn't have any problem forgiving him. I mean . . . I didn't forget what he did . . . I just had a better perspective on it. I think I got more out of that relationship than he did. Of course, if he ever gets his shit together, he would be great in politics. He has lots of good ideas, and he's the type of person who can put his thoughts into actions. But then again, he has so much internalized anger. He can't love anybody. He can't stand himself. I guess as long as he's going to Yale, and does well, his parents will think "all is fine."

As I mentioned before, Roger was my new love. At first, I loved him much more than he loved me. It just took him longer. I think Roger had trouble communicating at that level. I mean, to me, love is a timelessness . . . there is no separation. It was like a peak experience with Roger . . . I felt everything. It verified reality.

Roger had one sexual relationship before me. But he told lots of stories. He said that he had a Latin girlfriend, an Oriental girlfriend, and so on. They were his "friends," but not sexual friends. I didn't mind his stories, but I didn't understand why he wanted to make things up. I guess I never had that many confrontations with the male ego. Of course, Roger would tell these stories within the spirit of joking . . . and in this way, if you found him out, he would tell you that it was only a joke. But with me, he usually told the truth . . . and I could also tell when he was bullshitting.

My relationship with Roger was rather loud. Actually, it wasn't loud until I got pregnant. After that, there was a lot of pressure. I got pregnant because my IUD fell out, and I wasn't aware of it. Of course, even though my IUD fell out, I was still sure that I wasn't pregnant. I mean my period had been late before. But . . . it soon got obvious . . . I was getting sick in the morning, and it was a horrible time. I had edema to the point where I couldn't wear my shoes. I was nauseous. I had heat rashes . . . and all of the emotional stuff that goes with it. But, when I went for my urine test, it came back negative . . . saying that I wasn't pregnant. I knew that was bullshit, so I went to another doctor the next day. This time it came out positive. This doctor asked me if I wanted to keep the baby . . . and I said yes. But he told me that I couldn't do that . . . this IUD was taken off the market because it had a history of puncturing wombs. And the doctor wasn't sure whether all of it had come out. Since he couldn't find the strings, he didn't want to use an x-ray. Finally when he and his colleagues (he had four other doctors with him at this point) told me to sign release forms relieving them of responsibility if the baby died . . . I decided that I better get an abortion. It was a dreadful time. Roger and I both wanted a baby.

Having an abortion was not easy for me. I didn't think that I could go through with it . . . but I did. There was a big conflict within me . . . and I experienced a lot of bereavement afterwards. I didn't start feeling like myself again until four months later. And it really strained my relationship with Roger. There was a lot of friction between us . . . and if I can make this analogy . . . it was like very fine sandpaper . . . when you first rub it, it feels all right . . . but if you keep rubbing it, it will create a sore. Roger and I became sore . . . and different. Everything I did was insulting to Roger. And everything he did was terrible to me. He was so loud. He had such a bad temper . . . and he would break things. I remember he would drive and get mad at the tiniest things . . . and then speed up and knock over garbage cans. He was a monster when he was mad . . . and it was so unbearable for me.

It was then that we decided not to get married. Our families had actually met. I'll never do that again. Oh . . . it wasn't that bad. It was just uncomfortable. Roger's family is very middle class, and I think that they were overwhelmed by my grandparents' house in Beverly Hills. My grandparents throw their money around a lot. And Roger . . . and his father are very money conscious. It means a lot to them . . . and they don't have it. My grandfather also started talking business while Roger was in the room. And when he talks business . . . he is talking millions of dollars.

My grandfather made most of his money in the restaurant business. He owned a large chain of delicatessens. Some of the stores he sold to managers. Others he continues to run. This was very overwhelming for Roger . . . and I think my grandfather brought it up on purpose. Sometimes he would even take out a wad of hundred dollar bills. He could be very rude. I guess he wanted to show Roger how much power he had. My other boyfriends used to cough at that kind of stuff . . . they usually came from wealthy or gifted families. But Roger was pressured by this . . . he was always trying to live up to my grandfather . . . or my other boyfriends for that matter. It was a difficult situation for Roger.

Actually . . . when Roger and I were thinking of getting married, my grandfather gave us a house. The house was in my mother's trust . . . and he offered us a very lucrative arrangement. We were to fix up the house . . . and we would inherit it when we got married. I was also getting a little money from my trust (I mentioned this in my letter to you) . . . about a thousand a month. You know . . . my grandmother told me that I shouldn't tell people how much money I have . . . but since I've told you all of these other things . . . I guess I can also tell you about the trust. It is over $500,000. I receive about $12,000 per year . . . and the taxes on this money are paid from a separate account. I also pay taxes on stocks and stuff like that. Of the $12,000 I receive each year, I spend a certain amount on rent, food, and gas . . . and then I save some each month . . . for emergencies. I also use the money for travel. Although $12,000 is not a large income, I live well. And if there is an emergency, I have $10,000 in a Swiss bank account. My grandparents created this during the summer I went to Switzerland.

I am not the only one who has a trust account. My sister, Karen, has one (at about $500,000), but she gets only $500 a month. My grandparents don't trust her with money. My mother also has a trust account which is well over $1,000,000. She will also inherit everything from my grandparents . . . but I don't know how much this is worth.

Oh yeah . . . I mentioned before that Roger and I got this house. We were also supposed to get a $25,000 present for getting married. That was to insure that Roger's graduate school would be paid for. Well . . . in return for the house . . . we were supposed to fix it up. This house was near the beach in Santa Monica, in a beautiful residential area. Anyway . . . my grandparents kept giving Roger blank checks to pay for repairs on the house. But Roger went bananas . . . and spent more on the house than he should have . . . over $60,000. I guess he wanted the "best of everything." Roger also paid himself a salary and hired a couple of his friends. But the salary amounted to only $6,000, for about six months work.

When Roger and I decided not to get married, we moved out of the house. But Roger kept working, in order to finish what he started. My grandfather didn't like this. He thought that Roger was stealing from him. (He used to think all of his managers were stealing from him too.) My grandfather actually got an attorney and had all of the books investigated. They didn't find anything wrong . . . other than that everybody spent too much money. Roger didn't steal anything, but to this day my grandparents think that he did. Actually, Roger had to sue them in small claims court to get the remainder of the $6,000.

This was a very trying time for Roger and I. This thing with my grandparents was very ugly. I saw a side of my grandfather and grandmother that I had never seen before. Splitting up with Roger was also not very easy. But to be quite truthful, I can't pinpoint my specific reason for parting. I was still very much in love with him, but I started to notice that this was not going to work. It took

> me a long time to get to this point . . . I was having
> strange dreams . . . migraine headaches . . . and so on.
> We had gotten to the point of almost sending out our
> wedding invitations. We had the rings, the church, the
> priest . . . all that garbage. But Roger started giving me
> ultimatums about getting married . . . "It's my way or the
> highway." It was the highway . . . I went to Europe with
> my grandmother and a friend.

The relationship with Roger lasted one and a half years. He was a naive and insecure guy, who benefited greatly from Sarah. She gave him "worldliness." He traveled, shared sexual exploits, tasted wealth, and had the promise of financial security. On the other hand, Sarah also profited. She had an honest-to-goodness "peach seed." Roger was a blustering man/boy, whom Sarah could cuddle, mold, and control. Together they traversed a variety of relationship milestones, including living together, supporting themselves, preparing for marriage, and confronting abortion. When the problems outweighed the benefits, they split up.

The promise of the house and financial security (plus the meeting of families) is testimony to the seriousness of Sarah and Roger's relationship. And in this regard, it differs from Sarah's previous relationships. Glen is a case in point. It was an incestuous (teacher/son/etc.) affair and improbable from the start. In contrast, Roger was a fellow college student, only slightly older, but infinitely less experienced. Their relationship was not unlike many other serious, but flawed college student romances. They were fortunate to separate at an opportune time, and were not encumbered by marriage and children.

As Sarah indicated, she sought rest and refuge in Europe. She continues:

> It wasn't easy to leave for Europe. When I told Roger I
> was going, he kept saying . . . "Go, if you get this oppor-
> tunity to go to Europe . . . Go."

At first I kept saying, "No . . . no . . . no" . . . , but I finally agreed to go. And he was furious. I never did learn what Roger means when he says something. Even now, I still have to extract it out of him.

Paris was hard for me. I hadn't traveled for a while, and I had jet lag. I don't think that I slept for three or four days. To pass the time, I met up with a friend I'd known from Zurich. He was now a math teacher in a high school in Paris. In retrospect, this meeting was a mistake . . . he was in such a strange place. It's funny, when he (Marc) was a student, all he ever did was bitch about his teachers. But now he is a teacher who can't stand teaching. He aspires to be a movie director, but he only writes immature scripts . . . and all of his movies are exclusively footages. Somewhere along the line, we had sex . . . which was also a mistake.

Marc never had sex before. He was a twenty-three-year-old virgin. But . . . it was he who initiated it. And the first time we got together, he couldn't get an erection . . . which was all right and understandable given the circumstances. But Marc felt like a failure. After this first time, there were no other problems. When he didn't get an erection, he spent most of the time examining my body. But he didn't know basic biology. I remember him telling me that a woman can't get pregnant unless she has an orgasm. He had other far-out ideas. It was all very amazing. But . . . I wasn't in love . . . and he was. He kept doing very dramatic things, like throwing himself into the ocean . . . beating his chest . . . and so on. It was ridiculous. I guess all of this happened when I told him that I was no longer interested in him . . . that I couldn't have sex with someone that I didn't love. It would be leading him on . . . and I didn't want to have that kind of a relationship. I guess part of the problem was that I was still overwhelmed with Roger . . . trying to deal with the guilt.

In some ways, Roger was a parent figure for me. Although he didn't *feel* like a parent, he did become my superego. But he wasn't a "good conscience." When he would get mad at me, he would call me a whore. I never thought I would have to face that. But . . . anytime he lost his temper, that is what he would say. And this was a real shocker, especially coming from somebody you love. I guess after Roger and Marc, I really needed someone to make me feel that I was all right . . . that I wasn't a rotten person. So I started spending a lot of time with my grandmother and her friend. Which was kind of strange, since I was so much younger than everybody . . . they were all in wheelchairs. Fortunately, we stayed in some beautiful hotels.

When my grandmother and I left Paris, we went to Zurich. Almost everybody spoke German, so I was kind of lost. Actually, I met some people who spoke French . . . but everything was still written in German. After Zurich, we went back to Paris. We stayed at the Hotel Ritz. My grandmother amused herself by playing bridge. I had a strange affair with a cardiologist (Claude).

Claude was a friend of my male psychologist (Michael). I was supposed to meet with Claude to pick up a tape for Michael. Claude had seen a picture of me, but I had no idea what he looked like. I guess I expected him to look like Michael . . . you know, substantial . . . businesslike. But he was none of this . . . he was the homeliest man that I have ever seen. He was just so pathetic-looking . . . like something you would find in Cambodia. But, to my surprise . . . I fell very much in love with him.

Claude was developing something called "Psychomystical measurement." I guess this is how he and Michael became friends. Claude was doing this testing in the hotel where my grandmother and I were staying, so I had arranged to meet with him. Actually, he was supposed to give me a tape of a piano concert. Claude's sister was a pianist, and Michael wanted a copy of the tape. But Claude said that we would have to take a ride so that we could listen to the tape on the car stereo. I thought this sounded a little suspicious . . . but I went anyway. However, there was so much noise from the street musicians that we went to his office to hear the tape. I was getting this very weird feeling . . . but I also felt that there was no reason to feel uncomfortable. And when I looked at Claude . . . I was able to erase the tension from my mind.

When we got back to his office, I noticed Claude was living there. His wife had just divorced him, and he didn't have the money to get his own place. Claude and I went into a back room, and I sat down. I expected Claude to sit at a proper distance. He didn't . . . he just plopped down right next to me. But I didn't say anything. I thought it was all my imagination . . . untill he grabbed my hands. He then said, "Let me look at your palms." It was really weird . . . I wasn't sure what was going on.

Well . . . after he took my palm, he started "reading" it. I told him that I didn't know that he read palms . . . and then he said he didn't . . . and proceeded to kiss me. And all of a sudden . . . I had a feeling just like in the movies . . . like a rose blossoming. I had a sensation in my chest . . . and he felt it too . . . he actually started blowing on my chest. It was very strange. I'm not even sure whether I "enjoyed" it . . . I was in such a state of shock. After this experience, Claude looked very different to me.

You know, my grandmother is very "looks" conscious. So when she first saw Claude, it was like "ugh." She thought he was just atrocious. But you know . . . she later told me that after being with him for a few minutes . . . she no longer noticed the ugly look. Everything was sort of transformed . . . it was like the whole atmosphere became more peaceful. Of course, he really isn't that atrocious-looking. I think part of it for me was that I expected such a different look. I guess I was very surprised. And he looks much better now . . . he has gained some weight . . . and he is no longer going through a divorce.

After my experience in Claude's office, I asked him if he ever did this kind of thing before. He told me no, but it still felt bizarre. Later that week we went to a little art colony in the mountains . . . and on the way back we stopped in his office and made love. I was really baffled by this . . . baffled that I let myself get into this situation . . . and baffled by how strongly it affected me. When I finally left Paris, I was crying the whole time. I knew how much I would miss him.

Claude wasn't happy either. He felt that he was the "heavy" because he initiated our relationship. As for me, I still can't forget him. Even when my grandmother and I left for Italy (before coming back home) . . . thoughts of him still plagued me. It's funny, I would have assumed that Claude and I were just "ships in the night" . . . but he still affects me. It wasn't just a "rebound" phenomenon after Roger.

When I was in Italy, I had this very powerful image. It was of a wife crying . . . because of a fire. Her husband and child were being burned in a holocaust . . ."

The interview concluded with Sarah's description of her flight home. On the following day, August 28, 1979, Sarah gave me written accounts of two dreams:

Early this morning I had a dream with Paul. I was at his home. I don't know exactly why I was there. There was a piano and instruction books in a corner of the dining room. Paul was learning to play the piano and had advanced to the same place I had with the flute. For some reason I was under the impression that it had taken him longer to get there than it had for me.

I don't think that I had come over with the intention to have dinner but somewhere along the line this had become understood. Paul was cooking in the kitchen and Lisa was studying in the bedroom. I was preparing to set the table but first asked Paul if it would be all right if I took off my clothes (I felt more at home working with my clothes off). He consented. Later while I was setting the table it occurred to me that setting the table in the nude in someone else's house might be rude, or at least a bit strange.

After setting the table I started to get dressed but only got as far as my shirt and tennis shoes. At the time I thought that this constituted being respectfully dressed for dinner while still being comfortable. As the three of us sat down to eat I remember being very impressed by the quality of the meal.

Another dream I had concerning Paul was in my old bedroom of my mother's house. It had been converted into his office. It was even stocked with computers. My bed was still in the room and I was lying on one end of it dressed like I was prepared for cold weather (coat, gloves, scarf, etc.). I had no intention of staying there very long so I wasn't taking off my coat.

While I was talking to Paul a secretary or someone of this general disposition handed to me a stack of my dreams and memoirs which had been read, changed, pulled apart and recorded. There were red markings all over the papers. The whole thing seemed a bit cold to me.

These dreams appear to symbolize the interview process. In the first dream, Sarah represents her feelings of closeness by envisioning herself in my home. Since the interview focused on many sexual issues, the dream is also laced with sexuality. The playing of musical instruments is often a symbol of sexual behavior. However, in this case, we are playing independently—perhaps in Sarah's recognition of our personal independence. Sarah's belief that it had taken me longer to "get there" is a disguised reference to her own enlightenment: not all relationships are meant to be sexual.

Throughout the interview, Sarah exposed herself to me. Not surprisingly, in the first dream, she also exposed herself. Furthermore, she exposed herself in my home, with my ex-wife present. And though she makes gestures of modesty, she is nonetheless exposed. Finally, her reference to the "quality of the meal" represents her feelings about the interview sessions. She enjoyed them—and was surprised by this fact.

The second dream is also testimony to our working relationship. Sarah expresses fears of depersonalization ("seemed a bit cold to me"), and concerns about being treated without affection ("I was prepared for cold weather"). However, our shared experience has "brought me into her family," as symbolized by the office in her mother's house. Again, there is the attempt to distinguish between an interview process (office, computers, etc.) and a sexual relationship (i.e., bedroom).

After receiving these two dreams, I did not see Sarah for one year. I received some postcards, such as the following (12/18/79) from Switzerland:

> This is the area where I went to school one summer. I am staying at my old school as a guest. Later this afternoon Michael (my ex-shrinko) will meet me. Then tomorrow morning Michael and I go to Le Centre des Hautes Etudes Tibetaines to pow-wow with some big mucky-mucks there. We then drive back to Geneva where I take a plane to London and the next day fly back to El Lay. You'll probably hear from me before you ever get this card. What the hell. This is the most easygoing European trip I've been on, but am looking forward to seeing all my weirdo friends back home. Sarah

Sarah apparently had begun working for her former psychologist as a research assistant. As is evident from the postcard, she seemed in pretty good spirits. This is in contrast to the trip she took with her grandmother, a trip during which she started a frivolous affair with a twenty-three-year-old virgin (Marc), only to terminate it shortly thereafter; fell in love with a homely cardiologist (Claude), reassuring me it was not a "rebound" phenomenon; and finally, feeling at her wits end, was unable to sort out her feelings. Although Sarah has had a long string of relationships, it has become important for her to be in love. Roger, Marc, and Claude shared many things in common. They were needy, ineffectual, and insecure men who saw Sarah as a source of salvation. Given the problems with each relationship, I assumed Sarah's next phase of insight would involve finding a more independent and nurturing man.

Sarah ended her interview with the following image: "It was a wife crying . . . because of a fire. Her husband and child were being burned in a holocaust." At the time (August 1979) the meaning of this imagery escaped me. One year later, it became clear. It was Sarah's strong desire to have a husband and child. She was tired of crying and of missing opportunities. The previous relationships did not work out, and she feared that her chances of meeting a suitable husband and having a child were receding. I came to this conclusion because the next time I saw Sarah (summer of 1980) she excitedly told me that she was both pregnant (with the expectation of keeping the child) and getting married. She had met someone very special, and wanted to extend a wedding invitation to me. I thanked her and congratulated her. As an aside, I mentioned that for the purposes of this book, I had changed her name to Sarah. She laughed and said, "That was the name I used when I was turning tricks."

I was not optimistic. Despite Sarah's effusions, I could not imagine her success as mother and wife. First, the circumstances for getting married (pregnancy) were less than idyllic. Secondly, it is stressful enough to marry someone, let alone have a family. And I just couldn't see how they would survive as a couple. Finally, I expected the worse of her fiance (Keith). The last time I had spoken to Sarah she was trying to get over Claude (and Roger before that). I expected more of the same. But, to my surprise, I was wrong.

Keith was a young stock broker. Blond hair, three-piece suits, and a Harvard graduate. He was a clean-cut young man, with a boyishly engaging face. He seemed stable, secure, and hard-working. The first time I met him was at the wedding. I debated about attending, but in the end decided that I could not miss the opportunity to meet the cast of characters Sarah had so vividly described. Fortunately, nothing was ever mentioned about the book. I was introduced as a "former professor."

The wedding was in Malibu, at Keith's parents' home. It was an impressive, but tasteful estate overlooking the Pacific Ocean. Clear weather prevailed, so the ceremony was outside, with the bride and groom (and the audience behind them) facing the ocean. Two violins and a cello played Bach, and children gave out flowers. It was a relaxed but stately wedding.

All the cast (except Al) was there, with the most distinctive being Karen. She stood out like a sore thumb. Using a cane (she was only twenty-one years old), she hobbled around the grounds looking like a derelict bag woman. She hadn't washed for days, her hair was matted, her clothes dark and torn, and she never raised her eyes above the ground. It was obviously a difficult time for her, and perhaps she resented Sarah's being in the limelight.

I was better prepared for Sarah's mother and father since I had seen recent pictures of them. The hippy veneer was gone, and her father looked the part of a successful engineer (which he is). A dark three-piece suit, short hair, and a serious, but proud expression are his present "calling cards." He is still attractive and in very good shape. Sarah had shown me a recent picture of him playing tennis, resplendent in his Izod outfit.

Sarah's mother seemed uncomfortable. She was pleasant, but withdrawn. She was thin, had long, brown hair, and wore large glasses and nondescript clothing. She posed awkwardly for pictures with the bride, groom, and families.

Keith and Sarah were married by an elderly Indian man, dressed in what looked like a bright orange sari. He was the leader of an esoteric religious sect in Southern California. Sarah had met and befriended him, but was never a disciple. Keith seemed amused with this unusual master of ceremonies. The audience seemed aghast, especially Sarah's grandmother and grandfather (on her mother's side), who looked every bit like the wealthy Jewish grandparents they were. One other person of note was Sarah's former psychologist (Michael). He was a rotund, but dramatic-looking man, with a full, nicotine-stained, grey beard. No one could miss him.

Six months later, Sarah gave birth to a large, healthy baby girl.

At present, she is pregnant again, this one planned. In between, Keith and Sarah have prospered. They bought a house in the suburbs (with money from Sarah's grandparents). They spend their time refurbishing their home, and caring for their daughter. Keith's work has gone well, and Sarah is active in local politics. She also takes evening classes. I would like to report that she has finished her bachelor's degree, and is close to receiving her doctorate. But these are my achievement needs, not hers. She is happy, and is doing all she can to keep it that way.

I waited three years to write this book. I felt follow-ups were necessary before drawing conclusions. Sarah's circumstances may change, but enough time has now elapsed.

How did Sarah do it? I have several ideas, drawn from an existential framework, to explain how Sarah created meaning out of life. First, despite the abuse, Sarah was put in a leadership role. She was required to care for her sister, and, at different times, to care for her mother and father as well. She was the "strong" one, the person you count on when the "going gets rough." Unfortunately, the going was persistently rough and the circumstances were extremely traumatic, thereby setting up Sarah's strong need to rebel.

This situation created a young girl who was proud of her warmth and independence, yet was traumatized, angry, and self-destructive. She had alternating theories about the trauma: A) she was "tainted" and deserved what she got; and B) she had unbelievably bad luck. When she felt the former, she was despairing. When she attributed her lot to bad luck, she kept giving herself another chance, thereby creating a strong need to survive. The rest of the world was not like this, and with perseverance she would find those better people.

Finding people was easy for Sarah. She was extroverted and enjoyed her interactions. Some psychologists believe that extroversion is biological; others believe that it is learned. Whatever the case, Sarah profited greatly from this personality style.

Finally, Sarah's intelligence, attractiveness, and financial security can not be underestimated. People were drawn to her because she is a bright, articulate, interesting, *and wealthy* young woman. Moreover, she could afford to take care of herself, with psychotherapy, vacations, and independent living. Consequently, despite the setbacks, new opportunities were available.

Is Sarah unusual? She is very unusual. She is a unique case of psychological survival. Sarah is not the first victim of incest; the first adolescent prostitute; the first promiscuous teenager; the first bisexual; or the first self-destructive young person (and so on). She has been all of those things combined, but has found the ability to survive, adjust, and grow. Karen is more typical of the consequences of such abuse. She is traumatized, withdrawn, disturbed, and isolated—with little chance of rectifying her existence. Karen had many of the same advantages as Sarah (money, vacations, etc.), but lacked the unique set of assets and characteristics necessary to keep afloat. From Karen's point of view, why bother.

What can be learned from this case? First, money and education do not prohibit the sexual abuse of children. Victims come from all walks of life. Secondly, psychological survival is possible even in cases of abuse and tragedy. Victimized children can achieve successful adaptation as adults. It is certainly much harder, but there is no reason to conclude that adults are doomed by early childhood experiences. Sarah is a case in point. Her success can be attributed to her internal reorganization, and perception, of her previous experiences. She challenged the psychological meaning of such experiences and created an identity which minimized the trauma (attributing it to the vicissitudes of life), and maximized her assets (intelligence, wit, caring, etc.). Unfortunately, this is easier said than done. Most people do not have the opportunities, capabilities . . . or luck, that Sarah effectively used to her advantage.

Will Sarah live happily ever after? I do not know. The divorce rate is high; the recession is challenging financial stability; and Sarah's extended family offers little security. Even without a past as traumatic as Sarah's, no one is ever immune from problems and turmoil—so there are no guarantees. With good fortune and hard psychological work, Sarah could have a fighting chance.

AFTERWORD

To maintain Sarah's anonymity, I have changed her name and have avoided describing her. Instead, I have described family members, drawn from photographs and observations. To provide additional feedback, I have also asked two clinicians to give their impressions (from photographs) of the family members. This was done in the winter of 1979. Neither clinician (a clinical psychologist and social worker) was told anything about Sarah or the case. I merely asked them to judge the people from the photographs.

There are at least two biases in these descriptions. First, although no information was provided, the psychologist and social worker may have made a variety of assumptions about the photographs since they were drawn from a psychologist's file. Secondly, the photographs themselves may be misleading. A camera is a very reactive instrument, and as such, people behave *for* it. It is not clear whether a "personality style" captured on film is analogous to a personality style glimpsed off camera. With these cautionary remarks in mind, a composite of their descriptions follows.

Al (Stepfather): Very strange-looking, a low-life character; no morals; looks like a sociopath; vulgar. If you saw him on a street, you'd want to get away from him. Very threatening; if he smiled at a baby, the baby would cry. Extremely mean-looking face. Smiling doesn't come naturally. Also, crass, hard, greedy, no subtlety, insensitive."

Father: "Depressing. Loses sense of self from picture to picture.

Undergoes extreme changes. Seems unhappy with himself, trying to find a way to be. His uniqueness is 'I'm bizarre.' Nice-looking, seems to like costumes. San Fernando Valley cowboy. Prominent nostrils, large sculptured nose, dramatic face. Narcissistic, macho momma's boy. You could see him standing on a pier—tattooed. Looks like Evil Knieval. Cocky, and half sinister."

Mother: "Looks intellectual. Very masculine, with a large-featured face. Could be a man's face. She also looks like she could work in a bookstore or selling paintings. Looks a little like Woody Allen. A rich undirected person, searching for an identity, but not having one. Lost pseudo-intellectual."

Karen: "Chubby, baby-fat look. Bizarre, campy, underground character trying to act out compensatory fantasies. Profound inner emptiness. LSD feeling. She'd have you believe that she spends a lot of time at sex, drugs, and rock-'n'-roll parties. Sleazy glamour. Seems to flirt with incest and homosexuality, but there is also a denial of it. Possibly manic/depressive. Starved for attention, very needy and desperate. Doomed. Masochistic. The whole family seems to use being 'bizarre' to mean being 'special.' "

Sometimes, a picture is worth a thousand words.

EPILOGUE

It is now June 1983. I have allowed an additional eight months to elapse in order to obtain reviews of the preceding material, and to continue my contact with Sarah. During these eight months Sarah and I have had lunch twice, talked on the phone three times, and corresponded while I was giving a series of lectures at medical schools in Northern Italy. Keith, Sarah, and I also had dinner together at their home.

I remain firm in my belief that Sarah has made a remarkable recovery. Although a traditional lifestyle is *not* a prerequisite for psychological stability, it was very important to Sarah. She and Keith are a happy, traditional, upwardly mobile young couple. Sarah is a dedicated and able mother. She still harbors professional aspirations, but is also content with her domestic life. She cooks, cleans, and takes care of her young children. Before I left for Italy, she gave me some homemade cream liqueur, as well as a book to read on the airplane (Philip Garner's *Better Living Catalog*). Sarah has created a stable and fulfilling life, which is in sharp contrast to her early childhood.

At lunch one day, with her children crawling over both of us, I asked Sarah how she understood the dramatic change that had taken place in her life. First, she indicated that it was very difficult for her to identify with any of those previous experiences. She has had over three years of stability and has grown very accustomed to it. Offhandedly she also remarked that her horoscope emphasized "rebirth."

The intention of this epilogue is to provide a broader theoretical understanding of the transition in Sarah's life. Before developing this material, I will address several concerns raised by reviewers of this book.

Is Sarah anonymous? Every single name, place, profession, and so on has been changed. To further explain the extent of alteration would only detract from her well-protected anonymity. Moreover, the reader will note that there are no physical descriptions of Sarah. The cover drawing is Gayle Partlow's *feeling* of Sarah, created from Gayle's reading of the book. Sarah's husband is familiar with the book, a privilege which is shared with no other person.

Why did Sarah tell me her life story? One reviewer, in less than flattering terms, suggested that her interest in the publication of this material is motivated by "narcissistic, sadistic, and masochistic" tendencies. I feel differently. First, it is very difficult for me to pathologize Sarah, especially at this point in her life. Her tranquility and adjustment are a well-deserved respite from her childhood abuses. One may suggest that the process of this book is her unconscious, self-punitive attempt to undermine her happiness, but a more parsimonious explanation exists. The telling of her story, and the dramatic turnabout in her life occurred simultaneously, thereby suggesting that her motives were more like a purge than a punishment. Let us also not forget that Sarah's disclosures were made to a psychology professor at a major university. She did not peddle her tale to sensationalist journals or magazines. Moreover, this material is being published by a prestigious university press. If Sarah wanted to exploit the notoriety of her life, there are certainly more notorious avenues of expression. Finally, if there were secondary motives in Sarah's initial contact with me, they never surfaced. The contact she established was professional, and the relationship that ensued remained that way. If Sarah's motives were punitive, I believe that her selections would more adequately reflect that motive.

In the introduction of this book I indicated that my orientation is cognitive-existential. I will now explain this perspective. Cognitive psychology is the study of how we process or transform information about the world around us. Specifically, it is the study of how we organize, remember, and understand everything we experience. I recently applied this perspective to the study of human sexual behavior[1]. My intention was to develop a theoretical model which accounts for the types of experiences which are instrumental in creating sexual standards, as well as the types of sexual stimuli which routinely provoke sexual decisions. I hypothesized that all decisions regarding sexual expression are controlled by a hypothetical mechanism referred to as a *cognitive structure*. A cognitive structure does not really exist, it is a metaphor used to describe a reservoir of feelings and experiences. For instance, Sarah's sexual standards are a direct result of her collective experiences, although her present behavior may not reflect each specific instance. Instead, each instance leaves a memory residue. And it is these "residues" which are organized in a "cognitive structure" which regulates and controls sexual functioning. Furthermore, I believe that the memory residues are organized into a small set of principles, or codes of conduct, which determine how sexual stimuli are perceived and remembered. These principles are not static, but evolve as a consequence of continued experiences.

Sarah gives many examples of her sexual principles throughout this book: "I never thought of the incest as real sex . . . it was just something that was out there, but real sex was nice and a whole different thing"; "I didn't know that you were not supposed to masturbate in public"; "Eventually (I was around eleven or twelve) I decided to lose my virginity, which I saw as a nuisance"; "[sex between ages eleven and thirteen] to me, it was just a game—so I had a very playful attitude about it"; and so on. Each of these principles is a direct consequence of memory residues, and each is used by Sarah to regulate her sexual behavior. How did a young girl develop such principles? They are not surprising given the kind of sexual experiences she had. Her parents and stepbrother sexually abused her; she was raised in a very sexually permissive milieu; she was sexually precocious; and her sexual activity was often her only access to support and nurturance.

1. P. R. Abramson, "Implications of the sexual system," in *Adolescents, sex, and contraception,* ed. D. Byrne and W. A. Fisher (Hillsdale, N.J.: Erlbaum, 1983).

As I indicated previously, cognitive psychology examines how we process or transform information. I do not believe, however, that this approach alone is sufficient for understanding the broad spectrum of psychological phenomena. It does not acknowledge, or anticipate, the teleological qualities or psychological functioning. Consequently, I have combined both cognitive and existential psychology. I examine behavior in terms of how we organize, remember, and understand experience, with specific reference to how we create meaning in our lives. I have been particularly influenced by the work of Ernest Becker.[2]

I believe that children are active cognitively, and that they are also determined to extract meaning out of their world. As they grow older, broader existential issues prevail. How do I create meaning in life and try to live effectively even though I know I am going to die? How do I balance physical needs with spiritual needs? And so on. Sexuality becomes significant because it is a strong, forceful emotion which demands recognition, despite attempts to control or regulate it. At the cognitive level, sex is subject to countless incidences of learning. At the existential level, sex is a focal point in the balance between life and death, pain and pleasure.

Back to Sarah. As I indicated in this epilogue, Sarah's sexual principles are a direct consequence of her sexual experiences. However, the transition in her life is an existential phenomenon. It is testimony to her psychological growth and commitment. Although my interpretations have often been presented in a psychodynamic format, this perspective is consistent with both cognitive and existential psychology. While cognitive psychology may choose to study memory, what we remember and what we forget is often determined by dynamic emotional factors. Secondly, although existential psychology is concerned with how we extract meaning out of life, this does not preclude the importance of dynamic factors governing our day-to-day existence.

Sarah's remarkable recovery is best understood as an existential transition. Sarah's assertiveness, extroversion, and so on, were the

2. E. Becker, *The denial of death* (New York: Free Press, 1973).

tools. A change in commitment was the guiding force. Let me explain. Sarah was in the process of change from the moment she contacted me. For example, in her initial letter to me she quotes from the Chinese Book of Changes. She talks about the symbolic meaning of her birthdate: "the winter solstice 'brings the victory of light,' and the new moon marks also the end of darkness and the waning of light. They are symbolic turning points." It was a time of purging. She was twenty-one years old, another turning point.

In between the abuse and self-destructive behaviors, Sarah emerges as an active, striving individual. Even as a child, Sarah is actively telling her mother to leave. Sarah does not give up—she is appalled, angry, depressed, and confused, but she keeps fighting to maintain her integrity. This particular dilemma is her existential crisis: an attempt to resolve two opposing desires, establishing commitment versus succumbing to self-destruction. Was it necessary to relate Sarah's story in such explicit detail? I believe that the reader could not appreciate the enormity of the struggle if Sarah's words were not faithfully reproduced. We hear many stories about tragic souls. We are touched only momentarily because such stories are but fragments of reality. The complexity of tragedy cannot be understood without a full accounting. In Sarah's case, the abuse and trauma are exacerbated by her *own* self-destructive behavior. Her eventual recovery is preceded by *many* false starts. Is Sarah's stepfather the villain? Or is it the *combination* of Sarah's abusive stepfather and her passive mother? As the story expands, the picture grows clearer.

Sarah's resolution is the culmination of years of debate. She was moral to the extent that she actively examined all of her experiences, regardless of how ill-advised they may have been. She gives considerable evidence of introspection, constantly trying to solve her dilemma. Sarah also exhibits a strong need to define herself. Taken together, these characteristics were essential to her resolution. She chose commitment, commitment to herself. If others have failed her, she still has one ally, Sarah. But she needed to stop the self-destructive behavior. You may have noticed that Sarah stopped many self-destructive behaviors at opportune times. She stopped taking drugs when the effects hurt her. She stopped prostitution when she almost got arrested. She left the "bisexual arena" when the turmoil became overwhelming. And at twenty-one, she stopped a self-destructive life style. Also, as part of her commitment, she no longer considered herself culpable. The tragedy of William Styron's *Sophie's Choice* is that Sophie remained a slave to her "sin." Sarah found forgiveness; most importantly, she forgave herself.

What is the value of this book? It is a symbol of hope. Abuse, trauma, and turmoil exact an enormous psychological toll. But the ultimate destruction of the individual is the absence of hope. The resolution of Sarah's existential dilemma was the emergence of faith in herself. This book is significant to the extent that it documents psychological resolution in the face of endless abuse and trauma. Furthermore, it is the story of a real person. Sarah is by no means a hero. Her story has the potential to annoy, dismay, disgust, or excite. And it is *these* characteristics which make this an important case study. It is not pretty. It does not flow smoothly. Resolution is slow and questionable. There are no fireworks. But against all odds Sarah made it. Consequently, it offers hope to others.

INDEX

Printed in the United States
83826LV00002B/259-384/A